DIALOGUES CONCERNING NATURAL RELIGION

David Hume was born in Edinburgh in 1711, the second son of Joseph Hume, an advocate, and Katherine Falconer, daughter of an eminent lawyer who became Lord President of the Court of Session. He devoted himself from an early age to philosophy and literature and in 1739–40 published his now highly regarded work *A Treatise of Human Nature*. In his own words it 'fell dead-born from the Press' and he later reworked parts of the text. He applied for a professorship at the University of Edinburgh but was unsuccessful, largely due to local opposition. In 1746 he accepted a post as secretary to General James St Clair and was involved in a military campaign and, subsequently, in military embassies to Austria and Italy. By 1751 Hume had returned to Edinburgh. He was appointed librarian to the Faculty of Advocates, which gave him access to an extensive library. For the next twelve years he published a succession of works, which at last earned him an international reputation. During this time he wrote the first draft of the *Dialogues Concerning Natural Religion*. A complementary work, *The Natural History of Religion* appeared in 1757. His *Political Discourses* were published in 1752 and a six-volume *History of England* appeared between 1754 and 1762. In 1763 he was appointed private secretary to the British ambassador to France. On his arrival there he was greeted with adulation. He was briefly Under-Secretary of State in London before he retired to Edinburgh in 1769. Hume continued with his revision of the *Dialogues*, which were published posthumously in 1779. He died in 1776. Adam Smith said of Hume: 'I have always considered him, both in his lifetime and since his death, as approaching as nearly to the idea of a perfectly wise and virtuous man, as perhaps the nature of human frailty will admit.'

J. M. Bell was born in Nairobi in 1944. He was educated at Merchant Taylors' School, Northwood, and at King's College, Durham, the University of Newcastle Upon Tyne and Linacre College, Oxford. He has published on logic, on the philosophy of language and on Hume's philosophy in philosophical journals, and is co-editor of *Philosophy and Medical Welfare* (1988). Since 1969 he has taught philosophy at the University of York, where he is Senior Lecturer.

DAVID HUME

DIALOGUES CONCERNING NATURAL RELIGION

EDITED WITH AN INTRODUCTION
AND NOTES BY
MARTIN BELL

PENGUIN BOOKS

PENGUIN BOOKS

Published by the Penguin Group
Penguin Books Ltd, 27 Wrights Lane, London W8 5TZ, England
Penguin Books USA Inc., 375 Hudson Street, New York, New York 10014, USA
Penguin Books Australia Ltd, Ringwood, Victoria, Australia
Penguin Books Canada Ltd, 10 Alcorn Avenue, Toronto, Ontario, Canada M4V 3B2
Penguin Books (NZ) Ltd, 182–190 Wairau Road, Auckland 10, New Zealand

Penguin Books Ltd, Registered Offices: Harmondsworth, Middlesex, England

First published 1779
Published in Penguin Classics 1990
5 7 9 10 8 6 4

Material from Bayle's *Historical and Critical
Dictionary*, translated by R. H. Popkin,
is reprinted by kind permission
of Bobbs-Merrill Co. Inc., Inianapolis.

Material from Cicero's *De Natura Deorum: Academica*,
Vol XIX, translated by H. Rackham, is reprinted by permission of
the publishers and the Loeb Classical Library.
Cipyright 1933 by Harvard University Press

Printed in England by Clays Ltd, St Ives plc
Filmset in Sabon (Linotron 202)

CONTENTS

INTRODUCTION*

IN JULY 1776 James Boswell, the biographer of Dr Johnson, visited David Hume at his house in Edinburgh. Hume was suffering from the illness which led to his death seven weeks later. In his last months, he revised *Dialogues Concerning Natural Religion*, which he had written originally in the 1750s but had never published. But in many of the works published in his lifetime, he had discussed the nature of religious belief. Boswell knew the popular reputation Hume had as an unbeliever, and he was interested to see how he was facing death. In his journal[1] Boswell records that Hume told him that the morality of every religion was bad and that 'when he heard a man was religious, he concluded he was a rascal, though he had known some instances of very good men being religious'. Boswell was convinced both from what Hume said, and from his manner, which was calm and cheerful, that he 'persisted in disbelieving a future state even when he had death before his eyes'. Boswell found the interview disturbing:

I was like a man in sudden danger eagerly seeking his defensive arms; and I could not but be assailed by momentary doubts while I had actually before me a man of such strong abilities and extensive inquiry dying in the persuasion of being annihilated. But I maintained my faith. I told him that I believed the Christian religion as I believed history. Said he: 'You do not believe it as you believe the Revolution.'

The views about religion glimpsed in Hume's conversation with Boswell accord with his philosophical theories. In all his writings Hume argued that there is no reason to believe such doctrines as

---

* I would like to thank Christopher Bernard for his helpful comments on a draft of this Introduction.

that of the immortality of the soul; that religion is morally corrupting; that commonly ordinary men and women do not really believe what they profess to believe. Of course such views made enemies, and Hume's finest work on religion, the *Dialogues*, remained unpublished when he died largely because his friends had persuaded him not to publish it in his lifetime. Hume asked his close friend Adam Smith to supervise its posthumous publication, but he was unwilling, as was Hume's London printer, William Strahan. It appeared eventually in 1779, without a publisher's name, being brought to press by Hume's nephew who was following instructions in his uncle's will.

David Hume was born on 26 April 1711 in Edinburgh, the second son of Joseph Hume, an advocate, and Katherine Falconer, daughter of an eminent lawyer who became Lord President of the Court of Session. David did not know his father, who died in 1713. He was brought up by Katherine at the family estate, Ninewells, near the village of Chirnside a few miles from Berwick upon Tweed. He matriculated at Edinburgh University in 1723, it being common practice to go to college at a young age. After the usual course of study in Latin and Greek, ethics, mathematics, logic and natural philosophy (natural science) Hume returned to his family home. Not so commonly for the time, his study of natural philosophy had included some introduction to the theories of Sir Isaac Newton.

Katherine, to whom David was devoted, intended her younger son to follow family tradition and become a lawyer. But he preferred philosophy and literature, especially classical authors such as Cicero and Virgil. From the age of eighteen, he studied and thought with such intensity as to undermine his health. In eight years he developed the essentials of his thought, and wrote a philosophical masterpiece, the three-volume work called *A Treatise of Human Nature*.

In 1734 he left Ninewells and went to England, where for a few months he worked for a sugar merchant in Bristol. Abandoning this, he went to France, where he lived in La Flèche, in Anjou. Here there was a Jesuit college, at which René Descartes (1596–

1650) had been a student. In his correspondence, Hume says that in a discussion with a Jesuit in La Flèche he first constructed an argument against the credibility of stories of miracles, which he included in the *Treatise*. He completed the work in France, and in 1737, now aged twenty-six, went to London in search of a publisher. This was not altogether easy. While engaged in negotiations, Hume also planned to seek opinions of his work from leading thinkers. One of these was the theologian Dr Joseph Butler (1692–1752). Butler had recently published the *Analogy of Religion* (1736), but he was already familiar to Hume from his *Fifteen Sermons* (1726). Hume refers to Butler in the *Treatise* as someone whose thought influenced his own, and there are reasons to think that some of the theological views examined in the *Dialogues* were derived from Butler's writings. It was partly to avoid antagonizing Butler that Hume deleted from the *Treatise* the discussion of miracles.

The first two books of the *Treatise*, 'Of the Understanding' and 'Of the Passions', appeared in 1739, while the third book, 'Of Morals', was revised and published in 1740. That year Hume returned to Scotland. He was disappointed at the reception his book received, and soon began to think that he could do better at communicating his original and creative ideas, which were not understood. Most readers perceived the *Treatise* as full of paradoxes, absurdly sceptical, and a threat to established opinions about religion and morals. In 1744 Hume was encouraged to be a candidate for the Chair of Moral Philosophy at the University of Edinburgh. Opposition was mounted by some clergy and civic leaders, and pamphlets were written attacking him. Hume had taken a post as tutor to the Marquess of Annandale, who lived near St Albans. From there, he defended himself in *A Letter from a Gentleman to his Friend in Edinburgh* (1745) in which, writing in the third person, he summarizes his positive doctrines and replies to the charges of publishing wild and dangerous attacks on religion and morality. But his candidature for the university post failed.

Hume continued to write. He reworked some of the material from Book I of the *Treatise*, incorporated the essay on miracles, and published the result in 1748. Originally differently titled, this work is *An Enquiry Concerning Human Understanding*. Although the main philosophical ideas are the same in this book and in the *Treatise*, there are significant differences in style and structure which show a development in Hume's conception of the nature of philosophical argument. The implications of his epistemology (that is, his theory of the nature of belief and knowledge, reasoning and evidence) for religious belief are more explicit. Not only is there the discussion of the credibility of miracles, but there is a section which anticipates the *Dialogues* both in content and in literary form.

In 1746 Hume accepted a post as secretary to General James St Clair, who was to command a military expedition to Canada. St Clair's plans went astray, and his force eventually made an attack on the coast of Brittany. Hume's legal background led to his appointment as Judge Advocate in courts martial. In the following two years, he accompanied the general in military embassies to Vienna and Turin.

By 1751 Hume was back in Edinburgh. He was appointed librarian to the Faculty of Advocates, which gave him access to an extensive library. He was now at the height of his powers, and in the next dozen years published a succession of works, which at last earned him an international reputation. It was at this time that he first composed the *Dialogues*, together with a complementary work, *The Natural History of Religion*. This appeared in 1757, as one of *Four Dissertations*, which also included 'Of The Passions', the topic of Book II of the *Treatise*. Book III, 'Of Morals', was also restructured, appearing in 1751 as *Enquiry Concerning the Principles of Morals* – Hume believed that this was the best of all his writings. But in his lifetime Hume was probably better known for his political and historical writings than for his philosophy. (Yet it is a mistake to think of these as unconnected.) His *Political Discourses*, historically important in the development of both the conservative and liberal traditions, were published in 1752, and between 1754 and 1762 there appeared the six volumes of *History of England*. By the end of this period of his life, Hume was rich, famous, and still, in many minds, notorious.

At the end of the Seven Years War Hume was appointed private secretary to the British ambassador to France, Lord Hertford, and subsequently he was for a short time chargé d'affaires. His literary reputation in France was high. Most of his writings had already been translated, and reviews had been appearing for some years in European journals. As in Britain, Hume was praised for the clarity and elegance of his style, for his erudition, and for his powers of reasoning; but his scepticism and criticisms of religion were often condemned. Yet it is significant that he did not identify himself with the outright atheism of, for example, Baron d'Holbach.[2] His position was always sceptical rather than dogmatic.

After a brief further period of public service, this time as Under-Secretary of State, Northern Department, in London, Hume retired in 1769 to Edinburgh. He had a house built for himself in the New Town, in what was as a result jokingly called St David's Street. Here he lived until his death, devoting some of his time as was noted above to the revision of the manuscript of *Dialogues Concerning Natural Religion*, and making arrangements for its posthumous publication.

E. C. Mossner, author of the definitive modern biography of Hume and editor of the Penguin Classics edition of the *Treatise*, has written:

The *Dialogues concerning Natural Religion*, as an example of the philosophical dialogue, is beyond dispute the most brilliant in the English language, surpassing Berkeley's *Three Dialogues between Hylas and Philonous* (1713), the only serious contender . . . The *Dialogues* is the final marriage of philosophy with art that had been Hume's ambition throughout a long career as man of letters.[3]

Here we shall consider some of the main philosophical ideas they contain, and then look briefly at the literary style they exemplify, bearing in mind Mossner's comment, for the marriage of philosophy and art Hume achieves prevents us from interpreting them in a way that divorces content from style and structure.

The *Dialogues* are ostensibly a written record made by a young man, Pamphilus, of a conversation between three characters,

Cleanthes, Demea and Philo. Pamphilus, whose education is being supervised by Cleanthes, sends the account, with an introductory section and occasional interposed remarks of his own, to a friend, Hermippus. The Greek names of the characters, and the style and topics, show that Hume is adopting the technique of modelling his work on a classical original, in this case Marcus Tullius Cicero's *De Natura Deorum* (*On the Nature of the Gods*). Cicero examined in dialogue form the three main theologies then prevalent, the Epicurean, the Stoic and the Academic. Similarly, different conceptions of theology and the nature of religious belief are presented in Hume's work, and examined dialectically. The work is divided into twelve parts.

The first half of the eighteenth century was a period of intense debate in theology. One element was the writings of a group of thinkers known as deists. Deism was not a sharply defined position, but roughly it consisted of the view that all that it is necessary to believe in religion is what can be established about God, his purposes, and man's religious duty, by reason alone. Christian theologians had always drawn a distinction at some point between natural and revealed religion, that is, between what can be known of God by rational argument and what is to be accepted by faith as the special revelation of God in Christ. Faith was understood to be a response to truths revealed through the working of the Holy Spirit made possible by grace, a spiritual gift from God. However, it was also held that at least the existence of God, his nature as supreme creator, infinitely wise, powerful and benevolent, and his will that constitutes the moral law, could be known without revelation. And it was also common to hold that there can be evidence, acceptable to reason, that some religious teaching is part of God's revelation. Such things as the occurrence of miracles and the fulfilling of prophecies could be cited as evidence of Christ's divinity or of the inspiration and guidance of the church by the Holy Spirit. Scriptural authority for both the possibility of rational knowledge of God and for the necessity for salvation of the spiritual response of faith, could be found in St Paul. Almost universally, theologians cited The Epistle to the Romans, chapter 1, in support of the possibility of natural knowledge of God, and The First Epistle to the Corinthians, chapter 2, for the necessity of a spiritual response of faith.

Some deists rejected altogether the need for revelation and faith. Edward Herbert (1583–1648) in *De Veritate* (*On Truth*, 1624) had rejected the ideas of non-rational faith, an infallible church and the authority of priests as no part of 'true religion'. For him, true religion, purged of superstition, was a wholly rational affair consisting in an acceptance of 'common notions' that all men have. These are, that there is one supreme God; that he ought to be worshipped; that virtue and piety are the essence of worship; that we ought to be sorry for our sins and repent; and that God's goodness consists in his rewarding virtue and punishing vice in this world and the next. There is nothing especially Christian in Herbert's 'true religion', and he made an attempt, in *De Religione Gentilium* (*On the Religion of the Gentiles*, 1663) to show by a comparative discussion of ancient religions that all men at all times have accepted these beliefs.

Other deists hoped to show that Christianity, when properly understood, is also a wholly rational religion. They relied heavily upon reasoned argument, and drew some inspiration from the new science of Sir Isaac Newton (1642–1727) and Robert Boyle (1627–91). Arguments to prove the existence of God by appeal to the evidence of his 'general providence' displayed in the order of nature, and by more traditional reasoning based on the idea of God as a self-existent or necessary being, can be found in such works as *Christianity not Mysterious* (1696) by John Tolland (1670–1722), and *Christianity as Old as the Creation* (1731) by Matthew Tindal (1655–1733).

Many deists, then, held that religion is originally a rational response to the evidence of God's existence and providence displayed in nature, and that religious cults, rituals and mysteries, taking many forms and with proliferations of creeds, are all corruptions of the one true natural religion. Deism in this form was, in Hume's opinion, wholly mistaken. In *The Natural History of Religion* he argues against Herbert's attempt to show an original, rational monotheism at the base of all religions. The idea of divine providence, he says, does not in fact originate in a rational, detached admiration for the beauty and order of nature. Rather, religion originates in our emotional responses to the uncertainties of life, in our feelings of insecurity and vulnerability in a hostile world. Admiration of the regularity of the motion of the planets and appreciation of the divine wisdom increased by the discoveries of Galileo, Copernicus and Newton is not the common state of men's minds. Although the wise, who are concerned with theoretical explanation, may be led to the idea of a single supreme creator, the vulgar, ordinary men and women, are moved by

... the ordinary affections of human life; the anxious concern for happiness, the dread of future misery, the terror of death, the thirst for revenge, the appetite for food and other necessaries. Agitated by hopes and fears of this nature, especially the latter, men scrutinize, with a trembling curiosity, the course of future causes, and examine the various and contrary events of human life. And in this disordered scene, with eyes still more disordered and astonished, they see the first obscure traces of divinity.[4]

The contrast is between admiration of regularity and order on the one hand, and fear and anxiety in face of disorder on the other. Where the world appears, as it does to the vulgar, capricious and uncertain it is natural for the imagination to construct a number of deities, whose differing attributes and personalities can be invoked as appropriate. The ideas of the various gods arise from our ignorance by a process in which emotion, mediated by the imagination, leads to beliefs in deities that are constructions of the mind:

We are placed in this world, as in a great theatre, where the true springs and causes of every event are entirely concealed from us; nor have we either sufficient wisdom to foresee, or power to prevent those ills, with which we are continually threatened. We hang in perpetual suspense between life and death, health and sickness, plenty and want; which are distributed amongst the human species by secret and unknown causes, whose operation is oft unexpected, and always unaccountable. These *unknown causes*, then, become the constant object of our hope and fear; and while the passions are kept in perpetual alarm by an anxious expectation of the events, the imagination is equally employed in forming ideas of those powers, on which we have so entire a dependance.[5]

Thus polytheism rather than monotheism is the first form of natural religion.

It should be noted that in the *Natural History*, and elsewhere in his writings on religion, Hume is prepared to adopt a distinction between 'true' and 'false' religion. The origin of polytheistic beliefs in fears and hopes exemplifies what he calls 'superstition', and he is willing to regard this together with another form of religious belief originating in emotion, 'enthusiasm', as 'the corruptions of true religion', as 'two species of false religion'. There is thus a similarity here with the deists, who also regarded many forms of devotion and ritual as superstitious. Hume's list is:

... ceremonies, observances, mortifications, sacrifices, presents, or ... any practice, however absurd or frivolous, which either folly or knavery recommends to a blind and terrified credulity.[6]

But this similarity should not obscure from us his opposition to deism. The *Natural History* undermines the deist claim that 'true religion', in the form of something like Herbert's 'common notions', can be recommended on the grounds that it has always been accepted in all places. There is no argument for true religion based on the 'universal consent of mankind'.

A distinction between the true religion of the wise and the superstitions of the vulgar is found already in Cicero's dialogue on which Hume's work is modelled. There Cotta, the spokesman for the Academic school, says:

With the ignorant you get superstitions like the Syrians' worship of a fish, and the Egyptians' deification of almost every species of animal; nay, even in Greece they worship a number of deified human beings ... and with our own people Romulus and many others, who are believed to have been admitted to celestial citizenship in recent times, by a sort of extension of the franchise! Well, those are the superstitions of the unlearned; but what of you philosophers? How are your dogmas any better?

Hume, too, considers that to demonstrate that superstition and enthusiasm originate in ignorance, fear, hope, elation, flights of fancy and so on, is not to discredit true religion. The wise, the philosophers, may yet have grounds for a rational belief in a supreme creator and in the world as ordered and governed by divine providence. Are these dogmas any better? Is it possible to construct a rational natural theology, even if men and women are not generally led to religion by reasoning?

It is this question which is debated between the three characters in the *Dialogues*. Following Cicero's model, each character represents a different position on the central questions of natural theology. Can reason establish the existence of God? What can be known by reason of the nature and attributes of God? Can there be a reasoned solution to the conflict between divine goodness and divine power, given the existence of moral evil and natural suffering? What answer a philosopher or theologian gives to these questions is determined in part by his or her epistemology. It is necessary now to give an outline of a central aspect of Hume's own epistemology, as it is found in his earlier writings.

In the *Treatise* he argues that the fact that one phenomenon, or 'object' as he usually says, is the cause or effect of another is never something which is discoverable simply by reflecting on what is contained in our idea of it.[7] In order for us to know that fire burns us or bread nourishes us, we must experience the effect of fire or bread on our bodies. He expresses this by saying that we cannot have *a priori* knowledge of the causes and effects of objects. This contrasts, he thinks, with what holds in, say, mathematics. Here we can know that one object is related to another simply by abstract reflection. We can see that 16 is the square of 4 just by examining our ideas of these numbers. The necessary relations between numbers are thus relations *of ideas*; they are purely conceptual, and can be known *a priori*. One mark of truths which are relations of ideas is that the negations of such truths (e.g. that 16 is not the square of 4) are inconsistent and lead to a contradiction. In contrast, however certain we may be that fire burns us, we can imagine without contradiction a possible state of affairs (different from what actually obtains) in which we are not burned by fire. That fire burns us is thus simply a *matter of fact*, not an *a priori* necessary truth.

In the *Treatise* Hume therefore distinguishes between two

domains, relations of ideas and matters of fact. Using terms in a technical, philosophical sense, he calls the domain of relations of ideas *knowledge*, and the domain of matters of fact *probability*.[8] In this technical sense, it is a matter of probability that fire burns us. This does not mean, for Hume, that we cannot be certain that fire burns. Certainty is a matter of the degree of conviction that we feel about a thing, and we can be certain of something whose negation is still quite conceivable.

That we have beliefs about the causal properties of objects is itself a matter of fact. The question why fire burns us is a question for natural sciences – physics, chemistry, physiology – to answer. The question why we believe that fire burns us, however, is of a kind which, Hume thinks, has not previously been successfully answered. Evidently, that something is the case is not itself an explanation of why we believe that it is the case. The question of the origin of human beliefs is included in what Hume calls 'the science of man'. This science, the theory of human nature, is a foundation for all other sciences, both natural and moral. (By moral science or moral philosophy Hume does not mean just the study of morality, but also of politics, aesthetics, history.)

There is no question of importance, whose decision is not compriz'd in the science of man; and there is none, which can be decided with any certainty, before we become acquainted with that science. In pretending[9] therefore to explain the principles of human nature, we in effect propose a compleat system of the sciences, built on a foundation almost entirely new, and the only one upon which they can stand with any security.[10]

Hume's theoretical explanation of our beliefs about the causal properties of objects begins with his account of experience – it is from experience and not from *a priori* reflection that we discover that fire burns us. That is hardly news; but what gives Hume's account part of its distinctive character is his conception of experience. This conception has its origin in the thought of some of his predecessors, especially Descartes, Nicolas Malebranche (1638–1715), John Locke (1632–1704) and George Berkeley (1685–1753).[11] Experience is characterized subjectively, from the point of view of the person having the experience, and is a matter of the immediate content of consciousness. Our experience of fire, say, consists essentially in our having before our minds a *perception* of fire. Hume makes clear that his talk of perceptions in the mind as constituents of experience is part of a scientific theory. He says that 'the vulgar confound perceptions and objects'. Unreflective, ordinary men and women fail to distinguish between the fire and the perception of fire. They think that, in their experience of fire, the fire itself is a constituent of their consciousness and is, in some way, immediately before the mind. But here, as elsewhere, common assumptions and science diverge: '. . . philosophy informs us, that everything, which appears to the mind, is nothing but a perception.'[12]

Consciousness, for Hume, has two forms, feeling and thinking. When we feel, the warmth of the fire, the sensation of warmth, the sight of the flames, and the pleasure we get are all perceptions of the kind he calls 'impressions'. When we think, as now, of such a situation, the perceptions before our minds are called 'ideas'. Ideas, he argues, are copies of and originate from impressions. This aspect of Hume's theory has many ramifications. But one consequence is the denial that we can have ideas which, so to speak, go beyond the basis of impressions. This thesis is employed in the *Dialogues* by Philo to support the view that the nature of God is incomprehensible. Strictly speaking, we can have no *idea* of the divine nature:

Our ideas reach no farther than our experience. We have no experience of divine attributes and operations. I need not conclude my syllogism: You can draw the inference yourself.[13]

Although the content of our ideas cannot outrun the materials provided by experience, there is an obvious and important way in which we constantly think of things we have not experienced. If I see a child put her hand in the flame (I have that impression), I shall at once think that she will be burned (I have that idea). This idea, that she will be burned, is not derived from seeing her being burned. I think of what will happen before I see it happen. Anyone who has had the same kind of experiences of fire as I have had will do the same. This mental process (Hume calls it an 'operation of the mind') is a universal feature of human nature. It is essential to our life. It is a major task of the theory of human nature to explain this process. Hume regarded himself as the first person ever to do so successfully.

We must note at once that the question is not, why does fire burn? It is obvious that we all learn to make such inferences, from what we experience to what will happen next, long before we have any scientific understanding of the processes of nature. For Hume, what we do is to infer a cause or an effect (in the example, the effect of being burned) from an effect or a cause that we currently experience. Our capacity to perform these causal inferences does not depend upon our having a scientific theory of how the cause produces the effect. In most cases we are simply ignorant of the inner workings of nature. (In fact, Hume believes that we never can have any *ultimate* explanation of why things happen in nature as they do.)

It is also clear, he says, that we could never infer the effect of some cause we experience unless we had previously had experience of a relevant kind. Locke tells a story of an Oriental prince being told by a traveller from Europe that in his country, when it becomes very cold, the water in the canals becomes solid, so that it could bear the weight of an elephant. The prince replies that until then he had believed what the traveller told him of Europe, but now he knows that he is a liar. Hume, recalling the story, says, 'The Indian prince, who refused to believe the first relations concerning the effects of frost, reasoned justly.' Since the prince had no experience of the relevant kind of phenomena, he had no reason to believe that the effect of cooling water beyond a certain point is that it becomes solid. In no case, Hume argues, can we establish causal connections *a priori*.

It is previous experience of what Hume calls the 'constant conjunction' of causes and effects, and such experience alone, which enables us to 'reason justly' from causes or effects which we perceive to effects or causes which we do not perceive. This form of reasoning is quite distinct from *a priori* reasoning in the domain of 'knowledge', which is based simply upon relations between ideas. It is based on experience, and, being in the domain of 'probability', Hume calls it *probable reasoning*.[14] What the theory of human nature must do is explain how it is that experience of the conjunctions of causes and effects in our past experience leads to our being able to reason from a perceived phenomenon to its unperceived cause or effect. The essential feature of such reasoning, for which an explanation is required, is that what we *infer* is always a phenomenon *of the same kind* as those phenomena of which we have had previous experience. We always make inferences which presume that causal connections in nature are *uniform*. Why?

One possibility to be considered is that we make this presumption because we have a reason to do so. Hume thinks that this hypothesis cannot be correct. That causal connections between phenomena are uniform (that the same kind of cause always produces the same kind of effect) is not a necessary truth which we could have an *a priori* reason to believe. We can without contradiction imagine the negation being true – we can conceive a change in the course of nature. However, the only other sort of reason we could have would be to infer it from the evidence of past experience. We would then be inferring it by probable reasoning. But we were seeking an explanation of why probable reasoning has the character it has; and so it is circular to explain this by assuming probable reasoning already.

An alternative explanation, and the one which Hume favours, is that probable reasoning is not dependent on any other prior 'operation of the mind'; in fact, it is a kind of *instinct*. In the section of the *Treatise* called 'Of the Reason of Animals', he emphasizes the link he thus makes between this form of human reason and the instincts of other animals: 'To consider the matter aright, reason is nothing but a wonderful and unintelligible instinct in our souls.'[15] Although he here says that reason is an 'unintelligible' instinct, he does propose an account of the mechanism in the mind by which it operates. For the moment we can postpone outlining this. For the purpose of considering the *Dialogues* some other comments are needed.

As we have seen, Hume intended his theory of human nature to provide a foundation for other sciences:

Even *Mathematics*, *Natural Philosophy*, and *Natural Religion*, are in some measure dependent on the science of MAN; . . . 'Tis impossible to tell what changes and improvements we might make in these sciences were we thoroughly acquainted with the extent and force of human understanding, and cou'd explain the nature of the ideas we employ, and of the operations we perform in our reasonings.[16]

His account of the 'operation' of probable reasoning should, therefore, contribute to 'changes and improvements' in natural science and natural religion. The theory as summarized above applies initially to those inferences we make from causes and effects in everyday life, and these are characteristically immediate and unreflective. When I see the child put her hand in the fire, I infer at once that she will be burned. Although the inference arises from my past experience of the effects of fire, I do not even call this experience to mind. Hume recognizes, however, that we also make inferences of a more reflective nature. For example, when our experience is limited in extent, we proceed with more caution. We try to review what experience suggests. We begin to form what he calls 'general rules' to guide our more reflective reasonings. These form the basis of the even more elaborately reflective methodological principles of the natural scientist. One thing we then do is deliberately to seek experience of the conjunctions of phenomena, in experimentation. What the theory of human nature should do is enable us to recognize that the basis of a proper methodology, in any science, should be the natural workings of the human mind. That follows from the discovery that all reasoning is, in essence, a kind of natural instinct. In realizing this, we see what we can hope to achieve in any area. For example, we realize that we simply *cannot* discover natural laws in science by *a priori* reasoning. We understand that 'philosophical decisions are nothing but the reflections of common life, methodized and corrected.'[17]

As any natural theologian must, each character in the *Dialogues* assumes an epistemology. An epistemology not grounded in the theory of human nature is, for Hume, mistaken in itself, and therefore incapable of supporting conclusions in natural theology. Although both Demea and Cleanthes are made to employ principles drawn from Hume's own theory in criticism of the other speakers, Philo's methods of reasoning are the closest of the three to Hume's. By skilfully putting themes from his own philosophy into the mouths of his characters, and equally by having them also represent other types of philosophy opposed to his own, Hume aims to achieve the 'changes and improvements' which he considers so desirable in natural religion. He considers it especially desirable that his theory of human nature is applied to natural religion because the subject is not purely theoretical, but has a practical relation to how we should live.

In Part II, Cleanthes proposes a version of the Design Argument. He says that the argument is *a posteriori*, that is, from matters of fact established by experience, and that it is the only argument needed to prove both 'the existence of a deity and his similarity to human mind and intelligence'. An analogy can be seen between the structure of the world, and machines. The world resembles 'one great machine, subdivided into an infinite number of lesser machines'. As in a machine, the parts are 'adjusted to each other' with astonishing accuracy. In the case of machines, we know that the adjustment of parts to each other, and the 'adapting of means to ends', are caused by 'human design, thought, wisdom, and intelligence'. Since the ordered structure of a machine resembles the ordered structure of the world, and that of a machine is caused by intelligent design, we may infer 'by all the rules of analogy' that the cause of the ordered structure of the world is also intelligent design. As the structure of the world so much surpasses that of a machine, so, by analogy, the mind of the author of nature surpasses that of a man. He is proved to be 'somewhat similar to the mind of man, though possessed of much larger faculties, proportioned to the grandeur of the work which he has executed'.

In giving this argument, Cleanthes has claimed to be inferring a cause from an effect, and to be arguing analogically. But he has not, of course, given any detailed account of these principles of reasoning. By the device of having Philo suggest that Demea's vehement objection to the argument arises in part from his failing to see its logical structure, Hume introduces some of his own theory of such reasoning through Philo's 'restatement' of it. Philo paraphrases Hume to establish that 'experience alone can point out to [anyone] the true cause of any phenomenon'. It follows that whether or not such phenomena as 'order, arrangement, or the adjustment of final causes' are caused by design is something which can be established only by experience. If we consider only what is *a priori* conceivable, then it could be that the material world has a cause of its order inherent within it. Subtly, Philo brings out that Cleanthes must be assuming that the ideas in God's mind cause order in the world by themselves being ordered and structured, and similarly the ideas in the mind of a human being who makes a watch or a house 'arrange themselves so as to form the plan'. So Cleanthes is committed to the possibility of *some* things being inherently ordered. *A priori*, it could be matter as much as mind which has a cause of order inherent in it. So Cleanthes is claiming that it is from experience that we know that matter is not, but mind is, inherently ordered. Philo implies that all of this is already tacitly contained in Cleanthes' initial argument. By thus 'restating' it in terms of Hume's philosophy, Philo in fact identifies some of the weak points in it. But Cleanthes is invited to confirm that Philo has 'made a fair representation of it', and does so.

Throughout Part II Philo raises a series of difficulties with Cleanthes' method of argument, some of which are explored further in other parts. He objects, for example, that the analogy between the world and a machine is not close enough to permit the inference to design in the case of the world to be anything more than a conjecture. He points out that we know that design is a cause of order only in human activities, and these are a tiny part of the universe. Can we make such a small part a rule for the whole? He suggests that since the universe taken as a whole is a special, unique case, we simply have no relevant experience at all from which we could infer its cause. For himself, he says, so far as reason goes, he is content to say that he does not know what is the cause of the ordered, structured and purposeful world.

Hume's introduction of his own epistemology into the *Dialogues* as a critical weapon can be seen also in the case of Demea. From Part II to Part VIII, Cleanthes' design argument is thoroughly examined. As a result, it appears full of difficulties, and open to many doubts. Demea thinks such an argument, which Cleanthes asserted to be the only possible way to establish results in natural theology, is wholly inadequate as a basis for religious belief. In its place, he offers a 'simple and sublime argument *a priori*' which will be 'infallible'. This is a version of what is known as the cosmological argument. Whatever exists must have a cause or reason for its existence. In considering the series of causes of things, we must either think of this as going on in infinite succession, or we must think that there is an ultimate cause whose existence is *necessary*. But there cannot be an infinite series of things each of which is caused to exist by its predecessor and causes its successor to exist. For, if we consider the infinite series as a whole, it too must have a cause for its existence. (There could have been nothing at all rather than the whole infinite series.) *Ex hypothesi* there is no external cause for the whole infinite series. Nothing which is a member of the series can cause the whole. Consequently, it has no cause for its existence, which contradicts the premiss that whatever exists has a cause for its existence. 'We must, therefore, have recourse to a necessarily existent being who carries the *reason* of his existence in himself; and who cannot be supposed not to exist, without an express contradiction.'

This time it is Cleanthes who refutes the argument, employing Hume's principles. The essence of the refutation rests on the distinction between relations of ideas and matters of fact. Whether or not something exists is a matter of fact. Anything which is provable *a priori* is such that its negation is inconceivable. But whatever we think of as existing, we can equally think of as not existing. Therefore, there is nothing whose non-existence is inconceivable, and so nothing whose existence can be proved *a priori*. In fact, 'the words ... "necessary existence" have no meaning'. What Cleanthes says here is derived from Book I, Part III, Section VII of the *Treatise*. There Hume says:

'Tis evident . . . that the idea of existence is nothing different from the idea of any object, and that when after the simple conception of any thing we wou'd conceive it as existent, we in reality make no addition to or alteration on our first idea. Thus when we affirm, that God is existent, we simply form the idea of such a being, as he is represented to us; nor is the existence, which we attribute to him, conceiv'd by a particular idea, which we join to the idea of his other qualities, and can again separate and distinguish from them.[18]

When we form the idea that 16 is the square of 4, we have a complex idea which contains the component ideas of 16 and the square of 4. By reflecting on this complex idea, we see that the components must stand in the relation they do. But, if Hume is right about existence, when we think of something, and when we think of it as existing, there is no additional component idea of existence which is related to the idea of the thing. Consequently, it cannot be that by reflection we see that the idea of existence *must* be connected with the idea of the thing, because there is no separable idea of existence. Hence the words 'necessary existence' cannot stand for an idea. They have no meaning. Whether or not something exists is a matter of whether there is in reality anything corresponding to our idea; it is not a matter of what the *content of our idea* is.

The design argument given by Cleanthes is supposed to establish the existence of God, and something of his nature – that he possesses great wisdom, for example. The *a priori* argument given by Demea is also intended to prove the existence of a deity. But at the beginning of the *Dialogues* it is said that the existence of God is not in question; what will be discussed is the divine attributes, the nature of God. However, that there is no dispute about the existence of God is asserted initially by Pamphilus. Although all three characters are prepared to say that there is a God, they are not agreed about either what this means or whether it can be established by reason. Given Hume's view about existence, one could not believe that God exists without having an idea of God. So the distinction between questions about the existence and questions about the nature of God is shaky. Cleanthes holds that the design argument establishes similarity between God and human minds. This is attacked by both Philo and Demea. Demea's objection is that God is transcendent; he is beyond our comprehension. God's nature is a religious mystery. But, he says, the method of reasoning employed by Cleanthes suggests that we can understand the nature of God as analogous to our own. From his first statement of this position, in Part II, Demea expresses his position in religious rather than philosophical language:

Finite, weak, and blind creatures, we ought to humble ourselves in his august presence, and, conscious of our frailties, adore in silence his infinite perfections which eye hath not seen, ear hath not heard, neither hath it entered into the heart of man to conceive.

He goes on to quote from Malebranche's *De la recherche de la vérité* (*The Search after Truth*, 1674–5), in order to suggest that there is here harmony between reason and faith. This allows Hume to introduce into the *Dialogues* the notion of *anthropomorphism*, that is, the attribution to God of human characteristics. Philo and Demea then can use this term to summarize their criticism of Cleanthes. Demea regards the anthropomorphic notion of God generated by the design argument as not a proper object of religious devotion. In Part III, Cleanthes tries to support his argument with thought experiments – the examples of 'an articulate voice . . . heard in the clouds', and of a library of books which are 'natural volumes', not produced by mankind, but reproducing themselves 'in the same manner with animals and vegetables, by descent and propagation'. If there were such phenomena, he says, it would be absurd not to infer that they were the product of intelligence and design, for they would contain intelligible messages. He then draws an analogy with the actual structure of nature. (The idea of nature as a book, in which we can read the message of divine purpose, is an ancient one; it is found, for example, in the *Natural Theology* of Raymond Sebond, written around 1430.[19]) Demea objects that in reading a book we enter into the mind of the author, but we cannot enter into the mind of God. 'His ways are not our ways.' Besides, he says, the human mind, both in its *sentiments* and its *ideas* is wholly unlike the divine mind. Human sentiments, such as gratitude, love, pity, etc., 'have a plain reference to the state and situation of man'. And human thought is 'fluctuating, uncertain, fleeting, successive, and compounded'. But the God of faith cannot be thought to have sentiments or thoughts as we do.

In the main, however, it is left to Philo to develop the criticism of anthropomorphism. In Part V, he emphasizes that, insofar as Cleanthes is arguing from analogy, his conclusion will be better supported the more similar the inferred cause (of the order in nature) is to the known cause (of the order in machines). Thus the logic of Cleanthes' position pushes him into a more and more anthropomorphic conception of the mind of God. Cleanthes agrees with Philo that, for his argument, comparing divine and human intelligence, 'the liker the better'.

Philo exploits this in a series of arguments. He shows that the argument from analogy cannot establish any of God's attributes to be infinite, for 'the cause ought only to be proportioned to the effect'. Again, if we knew *a priori* that God is a perfect being, the imperfection in nature could be said to appear an objection only because of our limited understanding. (In Part X Demea expresses his faith that the wickedness and misery of mankind will at last be seen 'in some future period of existence' not to be inconsistent with divine power and benevolence. Cleanthes regards this as 'building entirely in the air'.) But if we are arguing *a posteriori*, then 'these difficulties become all real'. Furthermore, even if nature were perfect, the analogy with human design could suggest that the product results from trial and error: 'Many worlds might have been botched and bungled, throughout an eternity, ere this system was struck out.' Again, arguing from analogy cannot establish the unity of God. It would be even more analogous to human creation to suppose that so great a creation as the universe required the cooperation of a number of deities.

While Philo and Demea seek to make evident the incompatibility of Cleanthes' anthropomorphism with the religious idea of a single, transcendent, infinitely perfect God, Cleanthes attacks the idea that God's nature is incomprehensible as 'mysticism'. At the beginning of Part IV he asks how the thesis that the nature of God is incomprehensible differs from the view of 'sceptics or atheists' that the first cause is unknown. Similarly, in Part XI, he says that 'if we abandon all human analogy . . . I am afraid we abandon all religion, and retain no conception of the great object of our adoration.' Cleanthes is here as before depending on the empiricist account of the origin of ideas: that all our ideas must be derived from experience. Although Demea and Philo are initially made to appear in agreement, Demea is affronted by Philo's radical scepticism. Philo is concerned above all to establish a negative conclusion, that argument from analogy cannot yield the traditional view. Their divergence, hinted early in the *Dialogues*, becomes most apparent in Parts X and XI, which deal with the problem of evil.

Demea and Philo combine to paint a powerful picture of moral and natural evil. But Demea and not Philo thinks that in some way the imperfections of nature support religious belief. His attempt at arguing *a priori* having proved a failure, he now suggests:

that each man feels, in a manner, the truth of religion within his own breast; and from a consciousness of his imbecility and misery, rather than from any reasoning, is led to seek protection from that being, on whom he and all nature is dependent.

Philo gives to this a characteristically Humean twist. Nature appears unconcerned about the happiness of individuals, and to seek only the preservation of species. And while man can through society guard against many natural enemies, 'does he not immediately raise up to himself *imaginary* enemies, the demons of his fancy, who haunt him with superstitious terrors, and blast every enjoyment of life?' Demea's view, that men look to religion for consolation in the vale of tears, and believe that evil and suffering are, from the point of view of eternity, reconcilable with divine power and benevolence, is attacked by both Philo and Cleanthes. Philo remarks that the religious imagination is moved as much by fear as by hope. Cleanthes objects that Demea's position is entirely speculative.

Philo's principle target, however, is the possibility of *deriving* the moral attributes of God from the nature of the world. When Cleanthes presented the design argument, we were invited to 'look round the world', and to infer divine intelligence and design from its order and purpose. Here, where the attribute of divine benevolence is in question, Hume brilliantly balances Cleanthes' speech with Philo's:

Look round this universe. What an immense profusion of beings, animated and organized, sensible and active! You admire this prodigious variety and fecundity. But inspect a little more narrowly these living existences, the only beings worth regarding. How hostile and destructive to each other! How insufficient all of them for their own happiness! How contemptible or odious to the spectator! The whole presents nothing but the idea of a blind nature, impregnated by a great vivifying principle, and pouring forth from her lap, without discernment or parental care, her maimed and abortive children.

Philo claims that in arguing from nature to God, the mixture of good and evil to be found in nature prevents any inference to a wholly good, or wholly evil, cause of the universe. He allows that the idea of there being both a good and an evil principle has some probability, but rejects it on the ground of 'the uniformity and steadiness of general laws'; and consequently, he says, we are left with the idea of 'blind' nature – the cause or causes of the universe have no moral attributes at all. Earlier, in Part II, Philo had accepted that the existence of God is 'unquestionable and self-evident. Nothing exists without a cause; and the original cause of this universe (whatever it be) we call GOD; and piously ascribe to him every species of perfection.' Now he makes clear that the ascription of moral perfection to God can *only* be a matter of faith. So far as reasoning from the nature of the world goes, the most probable view is that God (i.e. whatever is the cause of the universe) has no moral nature. This conclusion is as unacceptable to Demea as it is to Cleanthes, who points out in Part X that 'there is an end at once of all religion. For to what purpose establish the natural attributes of the deity, while the moral are still doubtful and uncertain?'

These are some of the themes of the *Dialogues*. But there are others, also important to the question of the possibility of natural theology. I have not attempted a detailed analysis; for this there are a number of helpful studies, mentioned later. In any case, a systematic exposition of arguments, let alone a critical assessment, would not be in harmony with Hume's intention in writing in dialogue form. His general position about natural theology is sceptical, and his style is carefully adopted in order to achieve his sceptical aims. It is appropriate, therefore, to bear in mind some aspects of Hume's attitude towards scepticism.

Scepticism was a classical Greek philosophical method, taking various forms over a long period, from around 300 BC to about AD 220. At the end of this period, the aims and methods of the sceptics were summarized by Sextus Empiricus in *Outlines of Pyrrhonism*. This work appeared in translation towards the end of the sixteenth century, and from that time scepticism played a major role in the development of philosophy. Pyrrhonism, which takes its name from Pyrrho of Elis (*c*. 360–275 BC), was the most extreme form of scepticism; Hume sometimes calls it 'total scepticism'. Another source of knowledge of classical scepticism was Cicero's *Academica*, written in or after 45 BC. The Academy was the school of philosophy founded by Plato. Some considerable time after his death, scepticism was introduced and developed by successive heads of the school. Originally the scepticism of the Academy was total, but in time a more dogmatic position emerged, partly through the influence of the rival school of Stoicism. (Sceptics and Stoics are compared in Part I of the *Dialogues*.) One of those responsible for this was Philo, with whom Cicero studied scepticism when Philo was in Rome. Later, more full-blooded Pyrrhonism was revived, outside the Academy, and it is this later revival that is represented in the writings of Sextus Empiricus.

Just how Pyrrhonian and Academic scepticism differed is a matter of scholarship. But Cicero certainly suggests a difference, and Hume, from his study of Cicero, learned to use the terms 'Pyrrhonian' and 'Academic' to mark a distinction. Sceptical reflections often begin with the observation that the search for truth is frustrated by the disagreements found amongst men. Experts so often tell us different things; and even in common life we find that people's perceptions differ radically. When we are tossed about in the sea of conflicting opinions, the sceptic offers an escape to tranquillity of mind, by leading us to suspend our assent from any judgement. He does this, according to Sextus, by arguing both for and against any thesis in such a way that the issue seems undecidable. Faced with a balance between *pro* and *con*, the wise man does not commit himself either way.

Now Cicero implies that the Academic sceptics went so far towards committing themselves as to deny that knowledge can be achieved. (Sextus criticizes this as dogmatic.) And they were attacked by the Stoics, by the argument that if knowledge is impossible, then so is action. If we cannot know anything, we cannot know what to do. In response, the Academics formulated a notion of 'probability'. (The term in this context translates Cicero's '*probabile*', which in turn translates the original Greek expression.) The idea was that, although we have no sure criterion by which to sort truth from error, yet some things strike us as plausible or convincing, and, without committing ourselves to thinking that they are true, we can direct our actions by them. Probability is all we need, in practical terms.

Hume endorses this general position, and uses it to criticize the total scepticism of the Pyrrhonians. But his basis for the position is his own, and not anything he found in Cicero. It is to be found in his theory, already mentioned, that reason is a kind of natural instinct. On the one hand, this is a sceptical position. Hume denies that we can provide any antecedent justification for reasoning as we do from causes and effects. And, since that is so, we have no grounds for assuming that the conclusions we reach must be true. On the other hand, we do find ourselves, so to speak, persuaded by such inferences. Since it is our nature to reason as we do, there is no alternative. Hume's view here is much stronger than the classical sceptics. He is arguing that we cannot but think and reason as we do, not just that it is a practical policy to guide action by what seems probable. And, consequently, the idea of total scepticism, a total suspense of judgement, is a fantasy. There could be no such person as a total sceptic:

Nature, by an absolute and uncontroulable necessity has determin'd us to judge as well as to breathe and feel . . . Whoever has taken the pains to refute the cavils of . . . *total* scepticism, has really disputed without an antagonist.[20]

When Hume speaks of nature in these terms, he is taking a positive view of the convictions we find ourselves to have. But it is as much part of his complex theory of human nature that many beliefs arise in us which are not merely not known to be true, but positively absurd or harmful. In the *Treatise* he tries to separate the strong, irresistible and beneficial convictions which experience generates in the mind of the sceptical wise man (that fire burns, for example) from the fanciful, avoidable and often harmful notions that clutter the minds of the vulgar. Part of his theory is that powerful emotions often underlie the latter. We have seen that this diagnosis is important in his account of the origins of superstition and enthusiasm in religion.

The wise, who are enlightened by Hume's theory of human nature, know themselves better than do the vulgar. They can form general, reflective rules, based on the theory, by which to guard against the fictions of a lively imagination. In fact, it is the very process of reflection which diminishes the initial credibility of the ideas presented to us by emotion and imagination. So it would seem that the more reflective we are in our mental life, the better. But there is a twist in this. If we were to attempt to govern our beliefs entirely by reflective, general principles, we would end up without any beliefs at all – precisely the Pyrrhonian desideratum. For, as the sceptics showed, general principles of logic and methodology can always be set against one another so as to pull us in opposite directions. Hume's most considered view is that the beliefs of the wise man will be a vector of experience and reflection.

When Hume says that reason, in the sense of the capacity to

infer effects from causes and vice versa, is an instinct, he goes on to offer an account of how it operates. Very roughly, he thinks that we initially believe the evidence of our senses and memory, which give us vivid and forceful impressions. When we have had experience of the constant conjunction of two phenomena, such as fire and heat, the ideas of these become associated in the mind by a kind of conditioning. Hume calls this 'habit' or 'custom'. Then, whenever we have an impression of one of these phenomena, as when we see fire, the idea which is habitually associated with it, such as heat, immediately enters our consciousness. We see the child put her hand in the fire, and at once think that she will be burned. The belief we have in the evidence of our senses, which Hume identifies with the vividness and force of our perceptions, is transferred to the associated idea, and we believe that too. We do not merely think that she will be burned, we believe that she will. So belief itself turns out to be a naturally produced psychological state, which consists essentially in a kind of feeling: ideas which are the contents of belief *feel* strong, forceful and vivid.

It is because all this happens, he thinks, naturally and inevitably in everyday cases, like the example of the fire, that the Pyrrhonian idea that we might always suspend our assent, and have no beliefs at all, is absurd. This general position about how far it is possible to maintain a sceptical suspense of judgement is laid out at the beginning of the *Dialogues*, in the discussion between Cleanthes and Philo in Part I. But, very much in line with Hume's view, Philo claims that a sceptical suspense is possible where we are considering only abstract, reflective arguments. In those circumstances, the sceptic can always argue against the thesis being considered, so producing a weakening of conviction to balance the persuasive force of the original argument. If the topic is one on which we have no strong impulse to hold one view rather than another which results inevitably and unreflectively from past experience, then the dialectic of arguments for and against will lead to suspense of judgement:

All sceptics pretend that, if reason be considered in an abstract view, it furnishes invincible arguments against itself, and that we could never retain any conviction or assurance, on any subject, were not the sceptical reasonings so refined and subtle that they are not able to counterpoise the more solid and more natural arguments derived from the senses and experience. But it is evident, whenever our arguments lose this advantage and run wide of common life, that the most refined scepticism comes to be upon a footing with them, and is able to oppose and counterbalance them. The one has no more weight than the other. The mind must remain in suspense between them; and it is that very suspense or balance which is the triumph of scepticism.

Philo intends to show that in natural theology, our arguments do run wide of common life. But he is prepared to find himself convinced by very 'refined' and 'abstract' reasoning in, say, Newton's writings. Cleanthes therefore tries to show that religious belief can be supported by arguments of just the same kind as are used in science; hence the design argument. Philo's attacks are aimed at showing that the logic of the argument is *not* of the same type. Already by the end of Part VIII, he has achieved this aim. But at a number of places, and very clearly in Part XII, he accepts that it is, nevertheless, very natural to believe that the world is the creation of 'a first intelligent author'. What the sceptical technique does is to undermine the claim of the natural theologian that this natural assumption – what Cleanthes calls 'the religious hypothesis' – can be proved by reasoning of a kind employed in science, namely, analogical reasoning from effects to causes.

Apart from his own philosophy, Hume used a number of sources to construct the positions of his characters. As was mentioned earlier, Butler is one source for Cleanthes, in his use of analogical argument and his willingness to allow that probable reasoning is a proper method in natural theology. Demea's cosmological argument is based on sections of *A Demonstration of the Being and Attributes of God* (1705), by the influential theologian and Newtonian Samuel Clarke (1675–1729). And R. H. Hurlbutt has identified sources for parts of Cleanthes' speeches in two other Newtonians, George Cheyne (1671–1743) and Colin Maclaurin (1698–1746).[21] But it is, in my view, better to conceive of Hume's characters as representing *types* of theologians, rather than to think of them as standing each for a particular historical thinker. Of course, Philo's speeches far outweigh those of the others, both in quantity and in sophistication, and for the most part represent Hume's views. But Hume does enough, all the same, to give Philo some life of his own, particularly in the last Part. Here Philo expresses some elements of fideism:

A person, seasoned with a just sense of the imperfections of natural reason, will fly to revealed truth with the greatest avidity ... To be a philosophical sceptic is, in a man of letters, the first and most essential step towards being a sound, believing *Christian*.

This idea, that scepticism, by undermining the pretensions of reason, makes it possible for us to accept religious revelation by faith alone, has a long intellectual history. It would be perfectly familiar to Hume, not least from the writings of Pierre Bayle (1647–1706). But there is no doubt that Hume himself had no such tendency.

At the end of the *Dialogues*, Pamphilus judges that Cleanthes' principles are nearer to the truth than the others. This, too, is no guide to Hume's opinion. It echoes the ending of *De Natura Deorum*, where Cicero claims to have found that the theology proposed by the Stoic speaker 'approximated more nearly to a semblance of the truth' than the scepticism of the Academic spokesman. Since Cicero is identified in that work as one of the 'disciples of Philo, and have learned from him to know nothing', Hume is using the rhetorical device learned from his classical model. His intention in using the dialogue form is to avoid a direct statement of his position. He could well have had in mind Cicero again:

Those however who seek to learn my personal opinion on the various questions show an unreasonable degree of curiosity. In discussion it is not so much weight of authority as force of argument that should be demanded. Indeed the authority of those who profess to teach is often a positive hindrance to those who desire to learn; they cease to employ their own judgement ...

Additionally, the dialogue form enables Hume to practise the sceptical technique of balancing opposing arguments. According to his own theory of the nature of belief, this leads to a state of equilibrium, freeing the mind from dogmatism. This is illustrated most dramatically in Part XII, where Philo suggests that the end result of the discussion is a verdict so meagre in its content that whether we regard it as favouring theism or not is a purely verbal matter. But it is crucial, in Hume's eyes, that this minimal conclusion – *that the cause or causes of order in the universe probably bear some remote analogy to human intelligence* – is strictly a philosophical conclusion. It belongs to what Philo calls 'the philosophical and rational kind' of religion, and, as such, has no practical consequences whatever for how we ought to live our lives. And, of course, no sane man will think it worth the spilling of a single drop of blood. Hume consistently argued that where men and women hold religious beliefs as certain truths, regard all who do not share them as in error and seek to enforce religious practices, the consequences are always pernicious. But a purely theoretical examination of natural religion is, by its very inability to achieve results of any consequence, itself an antidote to the dogmatism and passion of popular religion. As Hume made his final revisions of the text of the *Dialogues* in the last months of his life, his judgement on the relation between religious conviction and philosophical investigation remained the same as it had been when he wrote the *Treatise* forty years earlier:

For as superstition arises naturally and easily from the popular opinions of mankind, it seizes more strongly on the mind, and is often able to disturb us in the conduct of our lives and actions. Philosophy on the contrary, if just, can present us only with mild and moderate sentiments; and if false and extravagant, its opinions are merely the objects of a cold and general speculation, and seldom go so far as to interrupt the course of our natural propensities . . . Generally speaking, the errors in religion are dangerous; those in philosophy only ridiculous.[22]

NOTES

(Further bibliographical details are given in the Select Bibliography, page 152.

1. (*p. 1*) Quoted in Kemp Smith, *Hume's Dialogues Concerning Natural Religion*, Appendix A.
2. (*p. 5*) See E. C. Mossner, *The Life of David Hume*, Chapter 33.
3. (*p. 5*) 'Hume and the Legacy of the Dialogues' in G. P. Morice (ed.), *David Hume: Bicentenary Papers* (Edinburgh, 1977), p. 2. For Mossner's biography of Hume, see preceding note. Details of the work by Berkeley, and of Mossner's edition of the *Treatise*, are given in the Select Bibliography. All references of the form 'T.*n*' are to page *n* of the Penguin Classics edition of the *Treatise*.
4. (*p. 8*) *The Natural History of Religion*, Section II.
5. (*p. 8*) Ibid., Section III.
6. (*p. 9*) 'Of Superstition and Enthusiasm' in *Essays: Moral, Political and Literary*.
7. (*p. 10*) 'There is no object, which implies the existence of any other if we consider these objects in themselves, and never look beyond the ideas which we form of them. Such an inference wou'd amount to knowledge, and wou'd imply the absolute contradiction and impossibility of conceiving any thing different.' T. 135.
8. (*p. 11*) *Treatise*, Book I, Part III, Section I, 'Of knowledge', Section II, 'Of probability; and of the idea of cause and effect'.
9. (*p. 11*) In Hume's writings, including the *Dialogues*, the word 'pretend' is commonly used to mean 'propose', 'claim', 'offer for consideration'.
10. (*p. 11*) T.43.
11. (*p. 11*) In a letter of 1737, Hume advised a friend to read works by Malebranche, Berkeley, Pierre Bayle (1647–1706) and Descartes, which 'will make you easily comprehend the metaphysical parts of my reasoning'. The letter does not mention Locke, but there is ample evidence of his influence on the *Treatise*. For the provenance of the letter and details of its publication, see R. H. Popkin, *The High Road to Pyrrhonism* (San Diego, 1980), p. 290. Modern editions of the works mentioned by Hume are listed in the Select Bibliography.
12. (*p. 12*) T.243.
13. (*p. 12*) See below, Part II, pp. 53.
14. (*p. 14*) *Treatise*, Book I, Part III, Section VI, 'Of the inference from the impression to the idea'.

15. (*p. 14*)   T.228.
16. (*p. 15*)   T.42.
17. (*p. 15*)   *An Enquiry Concerning Human Understanding*, Section XII, Part III.
18. (*p. 19*)   T.142.
19. (*p. 20*)   See the Introduction by M. A. Screech to Michel de Montaigne, *An Apology for Raymond Sebond* (Penguin Classics, 1987), p. xv.
20. (*p. 26*)   T.234.
21. (*p. 28*)   R. H. Hurlbutt, 'David Hume and Scientific Theism', *Journal of the History of Ideas*, 17, 1956, pp. 486–97.
22. (*p. 30*)   T.319.

TEXTUAL NOTE

THE present text is based on Hume's manuscript, with some modernization. In most instances where Hume uses an initial capital for a substantive, this text employs lower case; but there are exceptions, such as 'God'. Abbreviated forms such as 'tho' and 'convey'd' have been expanded: 'though', 'conveyed'. Spelling has been modernized; but for the most part Hume's punctuation is retained, since changes might affect the meaning.

Hume's own notes are signalled in the text by asterisks, and appear at the foot of the page. Editorial notes are signalled by superscript numerals, and are together after the text.

I am grateful to the Council of the Royal Society of Edinburgh for permission to use the manuscript, and to the staff of the National Library of Scotland for their help, and for making photocopies of the manuscript and of the so-called Second Edition, London, 1779.

DIALOGUES
CONCERNING
NATURAL RELIGION

PAMPHILUS to HERMIPPUS

IT has been remarked, my *Hermippus*, that, though the ancient philosophers conveyed most of their instruction in the form of dialogue, this method of composition has been little practised in later ages, and has seldom succeeded in the hands of those, who have attempted it. Accurate and regular argument, indeed, such as is now expected of philosophical inquirers, naturally throws a man into the methodical and didactic manner; where he can immediately, without preparation, explain the point, at which he aims; and thence proceed, without interruption, to deduce the proofs, on which it is established. To deliver a SYSTEM in conversation scarcely appears natural; and while the dialogue-writer desires, by departing from the direct style of composition, to give a freer air to his performance, and avoid the appearance of *author* and *reader*, he is apt to run into a worse inconvenience, and convey the image of *pedagogue* and *pupil*. Or if he carries on the dispute in the natural spirit of good-company, by throwing in a variety of topics, and preserving a proper balance among the speakers; he often loses so much time in preparations and transitions, that the reader will scarcely think himself compensated, by all the graces of dialogue, for the order, brevity, and precision, which are sacrificed to them.

There are some subjects, however, to which dialogue writing is peculiarly adapted, and where it is still preferable to the direct and simple method of composition.

Any point of doctrine, which is so *obvious*, that it scarcely admits of dispute, but at the same time so *important*, that it cannot be too often inculcated, seems to require some such method of handling it; where the novelty of the manner may compensate the triteness of the subject, where the vivacity of conversation may enforce the precept, and where the variety of lights, presented by various personages and characters, may appear neither tedious nor redundant.

Any question of philosophy, on the other hand, which is so *obscure* and *uncertain*, that human reason can reach no fixed determination with regard to it; if it should be treated at all; seems to lead us naturally into the style of dialogue and conversation. Reasonable men may be allowed to differ, where no one can reasonably be positive: Opposite sentiments, even without any decision, afford an agreeable amusement: And if the subject be curious and interesting, the book carries us, in a manner, into company, and unites the two greatest and purest pleasures of human life, study and society.

Happily, these circumstances are all to be found in the subject of NATURAL RELIGION. What truth so obvious, so certain, as the *being* of a God, which the most ignorant ages have acknowledged, for which the most refined geniuses have ambitiously striven to produce new proofs and arguments? What truth so important as this, which is the ground of all our hopes, the surest foundation of morality, the firmest support of society, and the only principle, which ought never to be a moment absent from our thoughts and meditations? But in treating of this obvious and important truth; what obscure questions occur, concerning the *nature* of that divine being; his attributes, his decrees, his plan of providence? These have been always subjected to the disputations of men: Concerning these, human reason has not reached any certain determination: But these are topics so interesting, that we cannot restrain our restless inquiry with regard to them; though nothing but doubt, uncertainty, and contradiction have, as yet, been the result of our most accurate researches.

This I had lately occasion to observe, while I passed, as usual, part of the summer season with CLEANTHES, and was present at those conversations of his with PHILO and DEMEA, of which I gave you lately some imperfect account. Your curiosity, you then told me, was so excited, that I must of necessity enter into a more exact detail of their reasonings, and display those various systems, which they advanced with regard to so delicate a subject as that of natural religion. The remarkable contrast in their characters still further raised your expectations; while you opposed the accurate philosophical turn of *Cleanthes* to the careless scepticism of *Philo*, or compared either of their dispositions with the rigid inflexible orthodoxy of *Demea*. My youth rendered me a mere auditor of their disputes; and that curiosity, natural to the early season of life, has so deeply imprinted in my memory the whole chain and connection of their arguments, that, I hope, I shall not omit or confound any considerable part of them in the recital.

PART I

AFTER I joined the company, whom I found sitting in *Cleanthes'* library, *Demea* paid *Cleanthes* some compliments, on the great care, which he took of my education, and on his unwearied perseverance and constancy in all his friendships. The father of *Pamphilus*, said he, was your intimate friend: The son is your pupil, and may indeed be regarded as your adopted son; were we to judge by the pains which you bestow in conveying to him every useful branch of literature and science. You are no more wanting, I am persuaded, in prudence than in industry. I shall, therefore, communicate to you a maxim which I have observed with regard to my own children, that I may learn how far it agrees with your practice. The method I follow in their education is founded on the saying of an ancient, *That students of philosophy ought first to learn logics, then ethics, next physics, last of all the nature of the gods.* * This science of natural theology, according to him, being the most profound and abstruse of any, required the maturest judgement in its students; and none but a mind, enriched with all the other sciences can safely be entrusted with it.

Are you so late, says *Philo*, in teaching your children the principles of religion? Is there no danger of their neglecting or rejecting altogether those opinions, of which they have heard so little, during the whole course of their education? It is only as a science, replied *Demea*, subjected to human reasoning and disputation, that I postpone the study of natural theology. To season their minds with early piety is my chief care; and by continual precept and instruction and I hope too, by example, I imprint

* Chrysippus apud Plut: de repug: Stoicorum[1]

deeply on their tender minds an habitual reverence for all the principles of religion. While they pass through every other science, I still remark the uncertainty of each part; the eternal disputations of men, the obscurity of all philosophy, and the strange, ridiculous conclusions, which some of the greatest geniuses have derived from the principles of mere human reason. Having thus tamed their minds to a proper submission and self-diffidence, I have no longer any scruple of opening to them the greatest mysteries of religion, nor apprehend any danger from that assuming arrogance of philosophy, which may lead them to reject the most established doctrines and opinions.

Your precaution, says *Philo*, of seasoning your children's minds early with piety, is certainly very reasonable; and no more than is requisite, in this profane and irreligious age. But what I chiefly admire in your plan of education is your method of drawing advantage from the very principles of philosophy and learning, which, by inspiring pride and self-sufficiency, have commonly, in all ages, been found so destructive to the principles of religion. The vulgar, indeed, we may remark, who are unacquainted with science and profound inquiry, observing the endless disputes of the learned, have commonly a thorough contempt for philosophy; and rivet themselves the faster, by that means, in the great points of theology, which have been taught them. Those, who enter a little into study and inquiry, finding many appearances of evidence in doctrines the newest and most extraordinary, think nothing too difficult for human reason; and presumptuously breaking through all fences, profane the inmost sanctuaries of the temple. But *Cleanthes* will, I hope, agree with me, that, after we have abandoned ignorance, the surest remedy, there is still one expedient left to prevent this profane liberty. Let *Demea's* principles be improved and cultivated: Let us become thoroughly sensible of the weakness, blindness, and narrow limits of human reason: Let us duly consider its uncertainty and endless contrarieties, even in subjects of common life and practice: Let the errors and deceits of our very senses be set before us; the insuperable difficulties, which attend first principles in all systems; the contradictions, which adhere to the very ideas of matter, cause and effect, extension, space, time, motion; and in a word, quantity of all kinds, the object of the only science, that can fairly pretend to any certainty or evidence. When these topics are displayed in their full light, as they are by some philosophers and almost all divines, who can retain such confidence in this frail faculty of reason as to pay any regard to its determinations in points so sublime, so abstruse, so remote from common life and experience? When the coherence of the parts of a stone, or even that composition of parts, which renders it extended; when these familiar objects, I say, are so inexplicable, and contain circumstances so repugnant and contradictory; with what assurance can we decide concerning the origin of worlds, or trace their history from eternity to eternity?

While *Philo* pronounced these words, I could observe a smile in the countenance both of *Demea* and *Cleanthes*. That of *Demea* seemed to imply an unreserved satisfaction in the doctrines delivered: But in *Cleanthes*' features, I could distinguish an air of finesse; as if he perceived some raillery or artificial malice in the reasonings of *Philo*.

You propose then, *Philo*, said *Cleanthes*, to erect religious faith on philosophical scepticism; and you think, that if certainty or evidence be expelled from every other subject of inquiry, it will all retire to these theological doctrines, and there acquire a superior force and authority. Whether your scepticism be as absolute and sincere as you pretend, we shall learn by and by, when the company breaks up: We shall then see, whether you go out at the door or the window; and whether you really doubt, if your body has gravity, or can be injured by its fall; according to popular opinion, derived from our fallacious senses and more fallacious experience. And this consideration, *Demea*, may, I think, fairly serve to abate our ill-will to this humorous sect of the sceptics. If they be thoroughly in earnest, they will not long trouble the world with their doubts, cavils, and disputes: If they be only in jest, they are, perhaps, bad railers, but can never be very dangerous, either to the state, to philosophy, or to religion.

In reality, *Philo*, continued he, it seems certain, that though a man in a flush of humour, after intense reflection on the many

at the outset - Philo labeled as skeptic

contradictions and imperfections of human reason, may entirely renounce all belief and opinion; it is impossible for him to persevere in this total scepticism, or make it appear in his conduct for a few hours. External objects press in upon him: Passions solicit him: His philosophical melancholy dissipates; and even the utmost violence upon his own temper will not be able during any time, to preserve the poor appearance of scepticism.[2] And for what reason impose on himself such a violence? This is a point, in which it will be impossible for him ever to satisfy himself, consistent with his sceptical principles: So that upon the whole nothing could be more ridiculous than the principles of the ancient *Pyrrhonians*,[3] if in reality they endeavoured, as is pretended, to extend throughout the same scepticism, which they had learned from the declamations of their school, and which they ought to have confined to them.

In this view, there appears a great resemblance between the sects of the *Stoics*[4] and *Pyrrhonians*, though perpetual antagonists: And both of them seem founded on this erroneous maxim, that what a man can perform sometimes, and in some dispositions, he can perform always, and in every disposition. When the mind, by stoical reflections, is elevated into a sublime enthusiasm of virtue, and strongly smit with any *species* of honour or public good, the utmost bodily pain and sufferance will not prevail over such a high sense of duty; and it is possible, perhaps, by its means, even to smile and exult in the midst of tortures.[5] If this sometimes may be the case in fact and reality, much more may a philosopher, in his school, or even in his closet, work himself up to such an enthusiasm, and support in imagination the acutest pain or most calamitous event, which he can possibly conceive. But how shall he support this enthusiasm itself? The bent of his mind relaxes, and cannot be recalled at pleasure: Avocations lead him astray: Misfortunes attack him unawares: And the *philosopher* sinks by degrees into the *plebeian*.

I allow of your comparison between the *Stoics* and *Sceptics*, replied *Philo*. But you may observe, at the same time, that though the mind cannot, in Stoicism, support the highest flights of philosophy, yet even when it sinks lower, it still retains somewhat of its former disposition; and the effects of the Stoic's reasoning will appear in his conduct in common life, and through the whole tenor of his actions. The ancient schools, particularly that of *Zeno*, produced examples of virtue and constancy which seem astonishing to present times.

> Vain Wisdom all and false Philosophy.
> Yet with a pleasing sorcery could charm
> Pain, for a while, or anguish, and excite
> Fallacious Hope, or arm the obdurate breast
> With stubborn Patience, as with triple steel.[6]

In like manner, if a man has accustomed himself to sceptical considerations on the uncertainty and narrow limits of reason, he will not entirely forget them when he turns his reflection on other subjects; but in all his philosophical principles and reasoning, I dare not say, in his common conduct, he will be found different from those, who either never formed any opinions in the case, or have entertained sentiments more favourable to human reason.

To whatever length anyone may push his speculative principles of scepticism, he must act, I own, and live, and converse like other men; and for this conduct he is not obliged to give any other reason than the absolute necessity he lies under of so doing. If he ever carries his speculations farther than this necessity constrains him, and philosophizes, either on natural or moral subjects, he is allured by a certain pleasure and satisfaction, which he finds in employing himself after that manner.[7] He considers besides, that everyone, even in common life, is constrained to have more or less of this philosophy; that from our earliest infancy we make continual advances in forming more general principles of conduct and reasoning; that the larger experience we acquire, and the stronger reason we are endowed with, we always render our principles the more general and comprehensive; and that what we call *philosophy* is nothing but a more regular and methodical operation of the same kind.[8] To philosophize on such subjects is nothing essentially different from reasoning on common life; and we may only expect greater stability, if not greater truth, from our philosophy, on account of its exacter and more scrupulous method of proceeding.

But when we look beyond human affairs and the properties of the surrounding bodies: When we carry our speculations into the two eternities, before and after the present state of things; into the creation and formation of the universe; the existence and properties of spirits; the powers and operations of one universal spirit, existing without beginning and without end; omnipotent, omniscient, immutable, infinite, and incomprehensible: We must be far removed from the smallest tendency to scepticism not to be apprehensive, that we have here got quite beyond the reach of our faculties. So long as we confine our speculations to trade or morals or politics or criticism, we make appeals, every moment, to common sense and experience, which strengthen our philosophical conclusions, and remove (at least, in part) the suspicion, which we so justly entertain with regard to every reasoning, that is very subtle and refined. But in theological reasonings, we have not this advantage; while at the same time we are employed upon objects, which, we must be sensible, are too large for our grasp, and of all others, require most to be familiarized to our apprehension. We are like foreigners in a strange country, to whom everything must seem suspicious, and who are in danger every moment of transgressing against the laws and customs of the people, with whom they live and converse. We know not how far we ought to trust our vulgar methods of reasoning in such a subject; since, even in common life and in that province, which is peculiarly appropriated to them, we cannot account for them, and are entirely guided by a kind of instinct or necessity in employing them.

All sceptics pretend, that if reason be considered in an abstract view, it furnishes invincible arguments against itself, and that we could never retain any conviction or assurance, on any subject, were not the sceptical reasonings so refined and subtle, that they are not able to counterpoise the more solid and more natural arguments, derived from the senses and experience. But it is evident, whenever our arguments lose this advantage, and run wide of common life, that the most refined scepticism comes to be on a footing with them, and is able to oppose and counterbalance them. The one has no more weight than the other. The mind must remain in suspense between them; and it is that very suspense or balance which is the triumph of scepticism.

But I observe, says *Cleanthes*, with regard to you, *Philo*, and all speculative sceptics, that your doctrine and practice are as much at variance in the most abstruse points of theory as in the conduct of common life. Wherever evidence discovers itself, you adhere to it, notwithstanding your pretended scepticism; and I can observe too some of your sect to be as decisive as those, who make greater professions of certainty and assurance. In reality, would not a man be ridiculous, who pretended to reject *Newton's* explication of the wonderful phenomenon of the rainbow,[9] because that explication gives a minute anatomy of the rays of light; a subject, forsooth, too refined for human comprehension? And what would you say to one, who having nothing particular to object to the arguments of *Copernicus* and *Galileo*[10] for the motion of the earth, should withhold his assent, on that general principle, that these subjects were too magnificent and remote to be explained by the narrow and fallacious reason of mankind?

There is indeed a kind of brutish and ignorant scepticism, as you well observed, which gives the vulgar a general prejudice against what they do not easily understand, and makes them reject every principle, which requires elaborate reasoning to prove and establish it. This species of scepticism is fatal to knowledge, not to religion; since we find, that those who make greatest profession of it, give often their assent, not only to the great truths of theism, and natural theology, but even to the most absurd tenets, which a traditional superstition has recommended to them. They firmly believe in witches; though they will not believe nor attend to the most simple proposition of *Euclid*. But the refined and philosophical sceptics fall into an inconsistency of an opposite nature. They push their researches into the most abstruse corners of science; and their assent attends them at every step, proportioned to the evidence, which they meet with. They are even obliged to acknowledge, that the most abstruse and remote objects are those, which are best explained by philosophy.

Light is in reality anatomized: The true system of the heavenly bodies is discovered and ascertained. But the nourishment of bodies by food is still an inexplicable mystery: The cohesion of the parts of matter is still incomprehensible. These sceptics, therefore, are obliged, in every question, to consider each particular evidence apart, and proportion their assent to the precise degree of evidence, which occurs. This is their practice in all natural, mathematical, moral, and political science. And why not the same, I ask, in the theological and religious? Why must conclusions of this nature be alone rejected on the general presumption of the insufficiency of human reason, without any particular discussion of the evidence? Is not such an unequal conduct a plain proof of prejudice and passion?

Our senses, you say, are fallacious, our understanding erroneous, our ideas even of the most familiar objects, extension, duration, motion, full of absurdities and contradictions. You defy me to solve the difficulties, or reconcile the repugnancies, which you discover in them. I have not capacity for so great an undertaking: I have not leisure for it: I perceive it to be superfluous. Your own conduct, in every circumstance, refutes your principles; and shows the firmest reliance on all the received maxims of science, morals, prudence, and behaviour.

I shall never assent to so harsh an opinion as that of a celebrated writer,* who says that the sceptics are not a sect of philosophers: They are only a sect of liars. I may, however, affirm, (I hope, without offence), that they are a sect of jesters or railers. But for my part, whenever I find myself disposed to mirth and amusement, I shall certainly choose my entertainment of a less perplexing and abstruse nature. A comedy, a novel, or at most a history, seems a more natural recreation than such metaphysical subtleties and abstractions.

In vain would the sceptic make a distinction between science (Cleanthes) and common life, or between one science and another. The arguments, employed in all, if just, are of a similar nature, and contain the same force and evidence. Or if there be any difference

* *L'Art de penser*[11]

· 47 ·

among them, the advantage lies entirely on the side of theology and natural religion. Many principles of mechanics are founded on very abstruse reasoning; yet no man, who has any pretensions to science, even no speculative sceptic, pretends to entertain the least doubt with regard to them. The *Copernican* system contains the most surprising paradox, and the most contrary to our natural conceptions, to appearances, and to our very senses: Yet even monks and inquisitors are now constrained to withdraw their opposition to it. And shall *Philo*, a man of so liberal a genius, and extensive knowledge, entertain any general undistinguished scruples with regard to the religious hypothesis, which is founded on the simplest and most obvious arguments, and, unless it meet with artificial obstacles, has such easy access and admission into the mind of man?

And here we may observe, continued he, turning himself towards *Demea*, a pretty curious circumstance in the history of the sciences. After the union of philosophy with the popular religion, upon the first establishment of Christianity, nothing was more usual, among all religious teachers, than declamations against reason, against the senses, against every principle derived merely from human research and inquiry. All topics of the ancient Academics were adopted by the Fathers; and thence propagated for several ages in every school and pulpit throughout Christendom. The Reformers embraced the same principles of reasoning, or rather declamation; and all panegyrics on the excellence of faith were sure to be interlarded with some severe strokes of satire against natural reason. A celebrated prelate* too, of the Romish communion, a man of the most extensive learning, who wrote a demonstration of Christianity, has also composed a treatise, which contains all the cavils of the boldest and most determined *Pyrrhonism*. *Locke* seems to have been the first Christian, who ventured openly to assert, that *faith* was nothing but a species of *reason*, that religion was only a branch of philosophy, and that a chain of arguments, similar to that which established any truth in morals, politics, or physics, was always employed in discovering

* Monsr. Huet[12]

all the principles of theology, natural and revealed.[13] The ill use, which *Bayle*[14] and other libertines made of the philosophical scepticism of the Fathers and first Reformers, still further propagated the judicious sentiment of *Mr Locke*: And it is now in a manner avowed, by all pretenders to reasoning and philosophy, that atheist and sceptic are almost synonymous. And as it is certain, that no man is in earnest, when he professes the latter principle; I would fain hope that there are as few, who seriously maintain the former.

Don't you remember, said *Philo*, the excellent saying of *Lord Bacon*[15] on this head. That a little philosophy, replied *Cleanthes*, makes a man an atheist: A great deal converts him to religion. That is a very judicious remark too, said *Philo*. But what I have in my eye is another passage, where, having mentioned *David's* fool, who said in his heart there is no God,[16] this great philosopher observes, that the atheists nowadays have a double share of folly: For they are not contented to say in their hearts there is no God, but they also utter that impiety with their lips, and are thereby guilty of multiplied indiscretion and imprudence. Such people, though they were ever so much in earnest, cannot, methinks, be very formidable.

But though you should rank me in this class of fools, I cannot forbear communicating a remark, that occurs to me from the history of the religious and irreligious scepticism, with which you have entertained us. It appears to me, that there are strong symptoms of priestcraft in the whole progress of this affair. During ignorant ages, such as those which followed the dissolution of the ancient schools, the priests perceived, that atheism, deism, or heresy of any kind could only proceed from the presumptuous questioning of received opinions, and from a belief, that human reason was equal to everything. Education had then a mighty influence over the minds of men, and was almost equal in force to those suggestions of the senses and common understanding, by which the most determined sceptic must allow himself to be governed. But at present, when the influence of education is much diminished, and men, from a more open commerce of the world, have learned to compare the popular principles of different nations and ages, our sagacious divines have changed their whole system of philosophy, and talk the language of *Stoics*, *Platonists*, and *Peripatetics*,[17] not that of *Pyrrhonians* and *Academics*. If we distrust human reason, we have now no other principle to lead us into religion. Thus, sceptics in one age, dogmatists in another; whichever system best suits the purpose of these reverend gentlemen, in giving them an ascendant over mankind, they are sure to make it their favourite principle and established tenet.

It is very natural, said *Cleanthes*, for men to embrace those principles, by which they find they can best defend their doctrines; nor need we have any recourse to priestcraft to account for so reasonable an expedient. And surely, nothing can afford a stronger presumption, that any set of principles are true, and ought to be embraced, than to observe, that they tend to the confirmation of true religion, and serve to confound the cavils of atheists, libertines and freethinkers of all denominations.

laying groundwork —
Skepticism — pros + cons
Philo — practically speaking
(day-to-day "life") —
"common conduct" not
outwardly affected by
skeptical problems —
experience gives some solidity
But METAPHYSICAL
questions are
affected

PART II

I MUST own, *Cleanthes*, said Demea, that nothing can more surprise me, than the light, in which you have, all along, put this argument. By the whole tenor of your discourse, one would imagine that you were maintaining the being of a God, against the cavils of atheists and infidels; and were necessitated to become a champion for that fundamental principle of all religion. But this, I hope, is not, by any means, a question among us. No man; no man, at least, of common sense, I am persuaded, ever entertained a serious doubt with regard to a truth so certain and self-evident. The question is not concerning the BEING but the NATURE of GOD. This I affirm, from the infirmities of human understanding, to be altogether incomprehensible and unknown to us. The essence of that supreme mind, his attributes, the manner of his existence, the very nature of his duration; these and every particular, which regards so divine a being, are mysterious to men. Finite, weak, and blind creatures, we ought to humble ourselves in his august presence, and, conscious of our frailties, adore in silence his infinite perfections which eye hath not seen, ear hath not heard, neither hath it entered into the heart of man to conceive them.[18] They are covered in a deep cloud from human curiosity: It is profaneness to attempt penetrating through these sacred obscurities: And next to the impiety of denying his existence, is the temerity of prying into his nature and essence, decrees and attributes.

But lest you should think, that my *piety* has here got the better of my *philosophy*, I shall support my opinion, if it needs any support, by a very great authority. I might cite all the divines almost, from the foundation of Christianity, who have ever treated of this or any other theological subject: But I shall confine myself, at present, to one equally celebrated for piety and philosophy. It is *Father Malebranche*, who, I remember, thus expresses himself.* 'One ought not so much (says he) to call God a spirit, in order to express positively what he is, as in order to signify that he is not matter. He is a being infinitely perfect: of this we cannot doubt. But in the same manner as we ought not to imagine, even supposing him corporeal, that he is clothed with a human body, as the *Anthropomorphites* asserted, under colour that that figure was the most perfect of any; so neither ought we to imagine, that the spirit of God has human ideas or bears *any* resemblance to our spirit; under colour that we know nothing more perfect than a human mind. We ought rather to believe, that as he comprehends the perfections of matter without being material . . . he comprehends also the perfections of created spirits, without being spirit, in the manner we conceive spirit: That his true name is *He that is*,[20] or, in other words, Being without restriction, All Being, the Being infinite and universal.'

After so great an authority, *Demea*, replied *Philo*, as that which you have produced, and a thousand more, which you might produce, it would appear ridiculous in me to add my sentiment, or express my approbation of your doctrine. But surely, where reasonable men treat these subjects, the question can never be concerning the *being* but only the *nature* of the deity. The former truth, as you well observe, is unquestionable and self-evident. Nothing exists without a cause; and the original cause of this universe (whatever it be) we call GOD; and piously ascribe to him every species of perfection. Whoever scruples this fundamental truth deserves every punishment, which can be inflicted among philosophers, *to wit*, the greatest ridicule, contempt and disapprobation. But as all perfection is entirely relative, we ought never to imagine, that we comprehend the attributes of this divine being, or to suppose, that his perfections have any analogy or likeness to the perfections of a human creature. Wisdom, thought, design, knowledge; these we justly ascribe to him; because these

* Recherche de la Verite. Liv.3. Chap.9.[19]

words are honourable among men, and we have no other language or other conceptions, by which we can express our adoration of him. But let us beware, lest we think, that our ideas anywise correspond to his perfections, or that his attributes have any resemblance to these qualities among men. He is infinitely superior to our limited view and comprehension; and is more the object of worship in the temple than of disputation in the schools.

In reality, *Cleanthes*, continued he, there is no need of having recourse to that affected scepticism, so displeasing to you, in order to come at this determination. Our ideas reach no farther than our experience: We have no experience of divine attributes and operations: I need not conclude my syllogism: You can draw the inference yourself. And it is a pleasure to me (and I hope to you too) that just reasoning and sound piety here concur in the same conclusion, and both of them establish the adorably mysterious and incomprehensible nature of the supreme being.

Not to lose any time in circumlocutions, said *Cleanthes*, addressing himself to *Demea*, much less in replying to the pious declamations of *Philo*; I shall briefly explain how I conceive this matter. Look round the world: Contemplate the whole and every part of it: You will find it to be nothing but one great machine, subdivided into an infinite number of lesser machines, which again admit of subdivisions, to a degree beyond what human senses and faculties can trace and explain. All these various machines, and even their most minute parts, are adjusted to each other with an accuracy, which ravishes into admiration all men, who have ever contemplated them. The curious adapting of means to ends, throughout all nature, resembles exactly, though it much exceeds, the productions of human contrivance; of human design, thought, wisdom, and intelligence. Since therefore the effects resemble each other, we are led to infer, by all the rules of analogy, that the causes also resemble; and that the author of nature is somewhat similar to the mind of man; though possessed of much larger faculties, proportioned to the grandeur of the work, which he has executed. By this argument *a posteriori*,[21] and by this argument alone, do we prove at once the existence of a deity, and his similarity to human mind and intelligence.

· 53 ·

I shall be so free, *Cleanthes*, said *Demea*, as to tell you, that from the beginning I could not approve of your conclusion concerning the similarity of the deity to men; still less can I approve of the mediums, by which you endeavour to establish it. What! No demonstration of the being of God! No abstract arguments! No proofs *a priori*![22] Are these which have hitherto been so much insisted on by philosophers all fallacy, all sophism? Can we reach no farther in this subject than experience and probability? I will not say, that this is betraying the cause of a deity: But surely, by this affected candour, you give advantages to atheists, which they never could obtain, by the mere dint of argument and reasoning.

What I chiefly scruple in this subject, said *Philo*, is not so much, that all religious arguments are by *Cleanthes* reduced to experience, as that they appear not to be even the most certain and irrefragable of that inferior kind. That a stone will fall, that fire will burn, that the earth has solidity, we have observed a thousand and a thousand times; and when any new instance of this nature is presented, we draw without hesitation the accustomed inference. The exactly similarity of the cases gives us a perfect assurance of a similar event; and a stronger evidence is never desired nor sought after. But wherever you depart, in the least, from the similarity of the cases, you diminish proportionably the evidence; and may at last bring it to a very weak *analogy*, which is confessedly liable to error and uncertainty. After having experienced the circulation of the blood in human creatures, we make no doubt, that it takes place in *Titius* and *Maevius*: But from its circulation in frogs and fishes, it is only a presumption, though a strong one, from analogy, that it takes place in men and other animals. The analogical reasoning is much weaker, when we infer the circulation of the sap in vegetables from our experience, that the blood circulates in animals; and those, who hastily followed that imperfect analogy, are found, by more accurate experiments, to have been mistaken.

If we see a house, *Cleanthes*, we conclude, with the greatest certainty, that it had an architect or builder, because this is precisely that species of effect, which we have experienced to proceed from that species of cause. But surely you will not affirm, that the universe bears such a resemblance to a house, that we can with the same certainty infer a similar cause, or that the analogy is here entire and perfect. The dissimilitude is so striking, that the utmost you can here pretend to is a guess, a conjecture, a presumption concerning a similar cause; and how that pretension will be received in the world, I leave you to consider.

It would surely be very ill received, replied *Cleanthes*; and I should be deservedly blamed and detested, did I allow, that the proofs of a deity amounted to no more than a guess or conjecture. But is the whole adjustment of means to ends in a house and in the universe so slight a resemblance? The economy of final causes?[23] The order, proportion, and arrangement of every part? Steps of a stair are plainly contrived, that human legs may use them in mounting; and this inference is certain and infallible. Human legs are also contrived for walking and mounting; and this inference, I allow, is not altogether so certain, because of the dissimilarity which you remark; but does it, therefore, deserve the name only of presumption or conjecture?

Good God! cried *Demea*, interrupting him, where are we? Zealous defenders of religion allow, that the proofs of a deity fall short of perfect evidence! And you, *Philo*, on whose assistance I depended, in proving the adorable mysteriousness of the divine nature, do you assent to all these extravagant opinions of *Cleanthes*? For what other name can I give them? Or why spare my censure, when such principles are advanced, supported by such an authority, before so young a man as *Pamphilus*?

You seem not to apprehend, replied *Philo*, that I argue with *Cleanthes* in his own way; and by showing him the dangerous consequences of his tenets, hope at last to reduce him to our opinion. But what sticks most with you, I observe, is the representation which *Cleanthes* has made of the argument *a posteriori*; and finding that that argument is likely to escape your hold and vanish into air, you think it so disguised that you can scarcely believe it to be set in its true light. Now, however much I may dissent, in other respects, from the dangerous principle of *Cleanthes*, I must allow, that he has fairly represented that argument; and I shall endeavour so to state the matter to you that you will entertain no farther scruples with regard to it.

Were a man to abstract from everything which he knows or has seen, he would be altogether incapable, merely from his own ideas, to determine what kind of scene the universe must be, or to give the preference to one state or situation of things above another. For as nothing which he clearly conceives could be esteemed impossible or implying a contradiction, every chimera of his fancy would be upon an equal footing; nor could he assign any just reason, why he adheres to one idea or system, and rejects the others, which are equally possible.

Again; after he opens his eyes, and contemplates the world as it really is, it would be impossible for him, at first, to assign the cause of any one event, much less, of the whole of things or of the universe. He might set his fancy a-rambling; and she might bring him in an infinite variety of reports and representations. These would all be possible; but being all equally possible, he would never, of himself, give a satisfactory account for his preferring one of them to the rest. Experience alone can point out to him the true cause of any phenomenon.[24]

Now, according to this method of reasoning, *Demea*, it follows (and is, indeed, tacitly allowed by *Cleanthes* himself) that order, arrangement, or the adjustment of final causes is not, of itself, any proof of design; but only so far as it has been experienced to proceed from that principle. For aught we can know *a priori*, matter may contain the source or spring of order originally, within itself, as well as mind does; and there is no more difficulty in conceiving, that the several elements, from an internal un-known cause, may fall into the most exquisite arrangement, than to conceive that their ideas, in the great, universal mind, from a like internal, unknown cause, fall into that arrangement. The equal possibility of both these suppositions is allowed. But by experience we find (according to Cleanthes), that there is a difference between them. Throw several pieces of steel together, without shape or form; they will never arrange themselves so as to compose a watch: Stone, and mortar, and wood, without an architect, never erect a house. But the ideas in a human mind, we see, by an unknown, inexplicable economy, arrange themselves so as to form the plan of a watch or house. Experience, therefore, proves, that there is an orginal principle of order in mind, not in matter. From similar effects we infer similar causes. The adjustment of means to ends is alike in the universe, as in a machine of human contrivance. The causes, therefore, must be resembling.

I was from the beginning scandalized, I must own, with this resemblance, which is asserted, between the deity and human creatures; and must conceive it to imply such a degradation of the supreme being as no sound theist could endure. With your assistance, therefore, *Demea*, I shall endeavour to defend what you justly call the adorable mysteriousness of the divine nature, and shall refute this reasoning of *Cleanthes*; provided he allows, that I have made a fair representation of it.

When *Cleanthes* has assented, *Philo*, after a short pause, proceeded in the following manner.

That all inferences, *Cleanthes*, concerning fact are founded on experience, and that all experimental reasonings are founded on the supposition, that similar causes prove similar effects, and similar effects similar causes; I shall not, at present, much dispute with you. But observe, I entreat you, with what extreme caution all just reasoners proceed in the transferring of experiments to similar cases. Unless the cases be exactly similar, they repose no perfect confidence in applying their past observation to any particular phenomenon. Every alteration of circumstances occasions a doubt concerning the event; and it requires new experiments to prove certainly, that the new circumstances are of no moment or importance.[25] A change in bulk, situation, arrangement, age, disposition of the air, or surrounding bodies; any of these particulars may be attended with the most unexpected consequences: And unless the objects be quite familiar to us, it is the highest temerity to expect with assurance, after any of these changes, an event similar to that which before fell under our observation. The slow and deliberate steps of philosophers here, if anywhere, are distinguished from the precipitate march of the vulgar, who, hurried on by the smallest similitude, are incapable of all discernment or consideration.

But can you think, *Cleanthes*, that your usual phlegm and philosophy have been preserved in so wide a step as you have taken, when you compared to the universe houses, ships, furniture, machines; and from their similarity in some circumstances inferred a similarity in their causes? Thought, design, intelligence, such as we discover in men and other animals, is no more than one of the springs and principles of the universe, as well as heat or cold, attraction or repulsion, and a hundred others, which fall under daily observation. It is an active cause, by which some particular parts of nature, we find, produce alterations on other parts. But can a conclusion, with any propriety, be transferred from parts to the whole? Does not the great disproportion bar all comparison and inference? From observing the growth of a hair, can we learn anything concerning the generation of a man? Would the manner of a leaf's blowing, even though perfectly known, afford us any instruction concerning the vegetation of a tree?

But allowing that we were to take the *operations* of one part of nature upon another for the foundation of our judgement concerning the *origin* of the whole (which never can be admitted) yet why select so minute, so weak, so bounded a principle as the reason and design of animals is found to be upon this planet? What peculiar privilege has this little agitation of the brain which we call thought, that we must thus make it the model of the whole universe? Our partiality in our own favour does indeed present it on all occasions: But sound philosophy ought carefully to guard against so natural an illusion.

So far from admitting, continued *Philo*, that the operations of a part can afford us any just conclusion concerning the origin of the whole, I will not allow any one part to form a rule for another part, if the latter be very remote from the former. Is there any reasonable ground to conclude, that the inhabitants of other planets possess thought, intelligence, reason, or anything similar to these faculties in men? When nature has so extremely diversified her manner of operation in this small globe; can we imagine, that she incessantly copies herself throughout so immense a universe? And if thought, as we may well suppose, be confined merely to this narrow corner, and has even there so limited a sphere of action; with what propriety can we assign it for the original cause of all things? The narrow views of a peasant, who makes his domestic economy the rule for the government of kingdoms, is in comparison a pardonable sophism.

But were we ever so much assured, that a thought and reason, resembling the human, were to be found throughout the whole universe, and were its activity elsewhere vastly greater and more commanding than it appears in this globe: Yet I cannot see why the operations of a world, constituted, arranged, adjusted, can with any propriety be extended to a world, which is in its embryo-state, and is advancing towards that constitution and arrangement. By observation, we know somewhat of the economy, action, and nourishment of a finished animal; but we must transfer with great caution that observation to the growth of a foetus in the womb, and still more, to the formation of an animalcule[26] in the loins of its male-parent. Nature, we find, even from our limited experience, possesses an infinite number of springs and principles, which incessantly discover themselves on every change of her position and situation. And what new and unknown principles would actuate her in so new and unknown a situation, as that of the formation of a universe, we cannot, without the utmost temerity, pretend to determine.

A very small part of this great system, during a very short time, is very imperfectly discovered to us: And do we thence pronounce decisively concerning the origin of the whole?

Admirable conclusion! Stone, wood, brick, iron, brass, have not, at this time, in this minute globe of earth, an order or arrangement without human art and contrivance: Therefore the universe could not originally attain its order and arrangement, without something similar to human art. But is a part of nature a rule for another part very wide of the former? Is it a rule for the whole? Is a very small part a rule for the universe? Is nature in one situation, a certain rule for nature in another situation, vastly different from the former?

And can you blame me, *Cleanthes*, if I here imitate the prudent reserve of *Simonides*, who, according to the noted story, being asked by *Hiero, What God was?*, desired a day to think of it, and then two days more; and after that manner continually prolonged the term, without ever bringing in his definition or description?[27] Could you even blame me, if I had answered at first, *that I did not know*, and was sensible that this subject lay vastly beyond the reach of my faculties? You might cry out sceptic and railer, as much as you pleased: But having found, in so many other subjects, much more familiar, the imperfections and even contradictions of human reason, I never should expect any success from its feeble conjectures, in a subject, so sublime, and so remote from the sphere of our observation. When two *species* of objects have always been observed to be conjoined together, I can *infer*, by custom, the existence of one wherever I *see* the existence of the other: And this I call an argument from experience. But how this argument can have place, where the objects, as in the present case, are single, individual, without parallel, or specific resemblance, may be difficult to explain. And will any man tell me with a serious countenance, that an orderly universe must arise from some thought and art, like the human; because we have experience of it? To ascertain this reasoning, it were requisite, that we had experience of the origin of worlds; and it is not sufficient surely, that we have seen ships and cities arise from human art and contrivance . . .

Philo was proceeding in this vehement manner, somewhat between jest and earnest, as it appeared to me; when he observed some signs of impatience in *Cleanthes*, and then immediately stopped short. What I had to suggest, said *Cleanthes*, is only that you would not abuse terms, or make use of popular expressions to subvert philosophical reasonings. You know, that the vulgar often distinguish reason from experience, even where the question relates only to matter of fact and existence; though it is found, where that *reason* is properly analysed, that it is nothing but a species of experience. To prove by experience the origin of the universe from mind is not more contrary to common speech than to prove the motion of the earth from the same principle. And a caviller might raise all the same objections to the *Copernican* system, which you have urged against my reasonings. Have you other earths, might he say, which you have seen to move? Have . . .

Yes! cried *Philo*, interrupting him, we have other earths. Is not the moon another earth, which we see to turn round its centre? Is not Venus another earth, where we observe the same phenomenon? Are not the revolutions of the sun also a confirmation, from analogy, of the same theory? All the planets, are they not earths, which revolve about the sun? Are not the satellites moons, which move round Jupiter and Saturn, and along with these primary planets, round the sun? These analogies and resemblances, with others which I have not mentioned, are the sole proofs of the *Copernican* system: And to you it belongs to consider, whether you have any analogies of the same kind to support your theory.

In reality, *Cleanthes*, continued he, the modern system of astronomy is now so much received by all inquirers, and has become so essential a part even of our earliest education, that we are not commonly very scrupulous in examining the reasons, upon which it is founded. It is now become a matter of mere curiosity to study the first writers on that subject, who had the full force of prejudice to counter, and were obliged to turn their arguments on every side, in order to render them popular and convincing. But if we peruse *Galileo's* famous Dialogues concerning the system of the world,[28] we shall find, that that great genius, one of the sublimest that ever existed, first bent all his endeavours to prove, that there was no foundation for the distinction commonly made between elementary and celestial substances. The Schools, proceeding from the illusions of sense, had carried this distinction very far; and had established the latter substances to be ingenerable, incorruptible, unalterable, impassible; and had assigned all the opposite qualities to the former. But *Galileo*, beginning with the moon, proved its similarity in every particular to the earth; its convex figure, its natural darkness when not illuminated, its density, its distinction into solid and liquid, the variations of its phases, the mutual illuminations of the earth and moon, their mutual eclipses, the inequalities of the lunar surface, etc. After many instances of this kind, with regard to all the planets, men plainly saw, that these bodies became proper objects of experience; and that the similarity of their nature enabled us to extend the same arguments and phenomena from one to the other.

In this cautious proceeding of the astronomers, you may read your own condemnation, *Cleanthes*; or rather may see, that the subject in which you are engaged exceeds all human reason and inquiry. Can you pretend to show any such similarity between the fabric of a house, and the generation of a universe? Have you ever seen nature in any such situation as resembles the first arrangement of the elements? Have worlds ever been formed under your eye? And have you had leisure to observe the whole progress of the phenomenon, from the first appearance of order to its final consumation? If you have, then cite your experience, and deliver your theory.

agreed: GOD IS. debated: can we know WHAT GOD IS?

staking their territory-

Demea - theist - outside of human comprehension

Cleanthes- design analogy

PART III

HOW the most absurd argument, replied *Cleanthes*, in the hands of a man of ingenuity and invention, may acquire an air of probability! Are you not aware, *Philo*, that it became necessary for *Copernicus* and his first disciples to prove the similarity of the terrestrial and celestial matter; because several philosophers, blinded by old systems, and supported by some sensible appearances, had denied this similarity? But that it is by no means necessary, that theists should prove the similarity of the works of nature to those of art; because this similarity is self-evident and undeniable? The same matter, a like form: What more is requisite to show an analogy between their causes, and to ascertain the origin of all things from a divine purpose and intention? Your objections, I must freely tell you, are no better than the abstruse cavils of those philosophers who denied motion, and ought to be refuted in the same manner, by illustrations, examples, and instances, rather than by serious argument and philosophy.

Suppose, therefore, that an articulate voice were heard in the clouds, much louder and more melodious than any which human art could ever reach: Suppose, that this voice were extended in the same instant over all nations, and spoke to each nation in its own language and dialect: Suppose, that the words delivered not only contain a just sense and meaning, but convey some instruction altogether worthy of a benevolent being, superior to mankind: Could you possibly hesitate a moment concerning the cause of this voice? And must you not instantly ascribe it to some design or purpose? Yet I cannot see but all the same objections (if they merit that appellation) which lie against the system of theism, may also be produced against this inference.

turns Philo's argument (or tries) on its head

Might you not say, that all conclusions concerning fact were founded on experience: That when we hear an articulate voice in the dark, and thence infer a man, it is only the resemblance of the effects, which leads us to conclude that there is a like resemblance in the cause: But that this extraordinary voice, by its loudness, extent, and flexibility to all languages, bears so little analogy to any human voice, that we have no reason to suppose any analogy in their causes: And consequently, that a rational, wise, coherent speech proceeded, you know not whence, from some accidental whistling of the winds, not from any divine reason or intelligence? You see clearly your own objections in these cavils; and I hope too, you see clearly, that they cannot possibly have more force in the one case than in the other.

But to bring the case still nearer the present one of the universe, I shall make two suppositions, which imply not any absurdity or impossibility. Suppose, that there is a natural, universal, invariable language, common to every individual of human race; and that books are natural productions, which perpetuate themselves in the same manner with animals and vegetables, by descent and propagation. Several expressions of our passions contain a universal language: All brute animals have a natural speech, which, however limited, is very intelligible to their own species. And as there are infinitely fewer parts and less contrivance in the finest composition of eloquence than in the coarsest organized body, the propagation of an *Iliad* or *Aeneid* is an easier supposition than that of any plant or animal.

Suppose, therefore, that you enter into your library thus peopled by natural volumes containing the most refined reason and most exquisite beauty: Could you possibly open one of them, and doubt, that its original cause bore the strongest analogy to mind and intelligence? When it reasons and discourses; when it expostulates, argues, and enforces its views and topics; when it applies sometimes to the pure intellect, sometimes to the affections; when it collects, disposes, and adorns every consideration suited to the subject: Could you persist in asserting, that all this, at the bottom, had really no meaning, and that the first formation of this volume in the loins of its original parent proceeded not from thought and design? Your obstinacy, I know, reaches not that degree of firmness: Even your sceptical play and wantonness would be abashed at so glaring an absurdity.

But if there be any difference, *Philo*, between this supposed case and the real one of the universe, it is all to the advantage of the latter. The anatomy of an animal affords many stronger instances of design than the perusal of *Livy* or *Tacitus*: And any objection which you start in the former case, by carrying me back to so unusual and extraordinary a scene as the first formation of worlds, the same objection has place on the supposition of our vegetating library. Choose, then, your party, *Philo*, without ambiguity or evasion: Assert either that a rational volume is no proof of a rational cause, or admit of a similar cause to all the works of nature.

Let me here observe too, continued *Cleanthes*, that this religious argument, instead of being weakened by that scepticism, so much affected by you, rather acquires force from it, and becomes more firm and undisputed. To exclude all argument or reasoning of every kind is either affectation or madness. The declared profession of every reasonable sceptic is only to reject abstruse, remote, and refined arguments, to adhere to common sense and the plain instincts of nature; and to assent, wherever any reasons strike him with so full a force, that he cannot, without the greatest violence, prevent it.[29] Now the arguments for natural religion are plainly of this kind; and nothing but the most perverse, obstinate metaphysics can reject them. Consider, anatomize the eye: Survey its structure and contrivance; and tell me, from your own feeling, if the idea of a contriver does not immediately flow in upon you with a force like that of sensation. The most obvious conclusion surely is in favour of design; and it requires time, reflection and study to summon up those frivolous though abstruse objections, which can support infidelity. Who can behold the male and female of each species, the correspondence of their parts and instincts, their passions and whole course of life before and after generation, but must be sensible, that the propagation of the species is intended by nature? Millions and millions of such instances present themselves through every part of the universe; and no language can convey a more intelligible, irresistible meaning, than the curious adjustment of final causes. To what degree, therefore, of blind dogmatism must one have attained, to reject such natural and such convincing arguments?[30]

Some beauties in writing we may meet with, which seem contrary to rules, and which gain the affections, and animate the imagination, in opposition to all the precepts of criticism and to the authority of the established masters of art. And if the argument for theism be, as you pretend, contradictory to the principles of logic; its universal, its irresistible influence proves clearly, that there may be arguments of a like irregular nature. Whatever cavils may be urged, an orderly world, as well as a coherent, articulate speech, will still be received as an incontestable proof of design and intention.

It sometimes happens, I own, that the religious arguments have not their due influence on an ignorant savage and barbarian; not because they are obscure and difficult, but because he never asks himself any question with regard to them. Whence arises the curious structure of an animal? From the copulation of its parents. And these whence? From *their* parents? A few removes set the objects at such a distance, that to him they are lost in darkness and confusion; nor is he actuated by any curiosity to trace them farther. But this is neither dogmatism nor scepticism, but stupidity: a state of mind very different from your sifting, inquisitive disposition, my ingenious friend. You can trace causes from effects: You can compare the most distant and remote objects: And your greatest errors proceed not from barrenness of thought and invention, but from too luxuriant a fertility, which suppresses your natural good sense, by a profusion of unnecessary scruples and objections.[31]

Here I could observe, *Hermippus*, that *Philo* was a little embarrassed and confounded: But while he hesitated in delivering an answer, luckily for him, *Demea* broke in upon the discourse, and saved his countenance.

Your instance, *Cleanthes*, said he, drawn from books and language, being familiar, has, I confess, so much more force on that account; but is there not some danger too in this very circumstance, and may it not render us presumptuous, by making us imagine we comprehend the deity, and have some adequate idea of his nature and attributes. When I read a volume, I enter into the mind and intention of the author: I become him, in a manner, for the instant; and have an immediate feeling and conception of those ideas, which revolved in his imagination, while employed in that composition. But so near an approach we never surely can make to the deity. His ways are not our ways. His attributes are perfect, but incomprehensible. And this volume of nature contains a great and inexplicable riddle, more than any intelligible discourse or reasoning.

The ancient *Platonists*, you know, were the most religious and devout of all the pagan philosophers: Yet many of them, particularly *Plotinus*, expressly declare, that intellect or understanding is not to be ascribed to the deity, and that our most perfect worship of him consists, not in acts of veneration, reverence, gratitude, or love; but in a certain mysterious self-annihilation or total extinction of all our faculties.[32] These ideas are, perhaps, too far stretched; but still it must be acknowledged, that, by representing the deity as so intelligible, and comprehensible, and so similar to a human mind, we are guilty of the grossest and most narrow partiality, and make ourselves the model of the whole universe.

All the *sentiments* of the human mind, gratitude, resentment, love, friendship, approbation, blame, pity, emulation, envy, have a plain reference to the state and situation of man, and are calculated for preserving the existence, and promoting the activity of such a being in such circumstances. It seems therefore unreasonable to transfer such sentiments to a supreme existence, or to suppose him actuated by them; and the phenomena, besides, of the universe will not support us in such a theory. All our *ideas*, derived from the senses are confessedly false and illusive; and cannot, therefore, be supposed to have place in a supreme intelligence: And as the ideas of internal sentiment, added to those of the external senses, compose the whole furniture of human understanding, we may conclude that none of the *materials* of thought are in any respect similar in the human and in the divine intelligence. Now, as to the *manner* of thinking; how can we make any comparison between them, or suppose them anywise resembling? Our thought is fluctuating, uncertain, fleeting, successive, and compounded; and were we to remove these circumstances, we absolutely annihilate its essence, and it would, in such a case, be an abuse of terms to apply to it the name of thought or reason. At least, if it appear more pious and respectful (as it really is) still to retain these terms, when we mention the supreme being, we ought to acknowledge, that their meaning, in that case, is totally incomprehensible; and that the infirmities of our nature do not permit us to reach any ideas, which in the least correspond to the ineffable sublimity of the divine attributes.

PART IV

IT seems strange to me, said *Cleanthes*, that you, *Demea*, who are so sincere in the cause of religion, should still maintain the mysterious, incomprehensible nature of the deity, and should insist so strenuously, that he has no manner of likeness or resemblance to human creatures. The deity, I can readily allow, possesses many powers and attributes, of which we can have no comprehension: But if our ideas, so far as they go, be not just, and adequate, and correspondent to his real nature, I know not what there is in this subject worth insisting on. Is the name, without any meaning, of such mighty importance? Or how do you *mystics*, who maintain the absolute incomprehensibility of the deity, differ from sceptics or atheists, who assert, that the first cause of all is unknown and unintelligible? Their temerity must be very great, if, after rejecting the production by a mind; I mean, a mind, resembling the human (for I know of no other) they pretend to assign, with certainty, any other specific, intelligible cause: And their conscience must be very scrupulous indeed, if they refuse to call the universal, unknown cause a god or deity; and to bestow on him as many sublime eulogies and unmeaning epithets, as you shall please to require of them.

Who could imagine, replied *Demea*, that *Cleanthes*, the calm, philosophical *Cleanthes*, would attempt to refute his antagonists, by affixing a nickname to them; and like the common bigots and inquisitors of the age, have recourse to invective and declamation, instead of reasoning? Or does he not perceive, that these topics are easily retorted, and that *anthropormorphite* is an appellation as invidious, and implies as dangerous consequences, as the epithet of *mystic*, with which he has honoured us? In reality, *Cleanthes*, consider what it is you assert, when you represent the deity as similar to a human mind and understanding. What is the soul of man? A composition of various faculties, passions, sentiments, ideas; united, indeed, into one self or person, but still distinct from each other. When it reasons, the ideas, which are the parts of its discourse, arrange themselves in a certain form or order; which is not preserved entire for a moment, but immediately gives place to another arrangement. New opinions, new passions, new affections, new feelings arise, which continually diversify the mental scene, and produce in it the greatest variety, and most rapid succession imaginable.[33] How is this compatible, with that perfect immutability and simplicity, which all true theists ascribe to the deity? By the same act, say they, he sees past, present, and future: His love and his hatred, his mercy and his justice, are one individual operation: He is entire in every point of space; and complete in every instant of duration. No succession, no change, no acquisition, no diminution. What he is implies not in it any shadow of distinction or diversity. And what he is, this moment, he ever has been, and ever will be, without any new judgement, sentiment, or operation. He stands fixed in one simple, perfect state; nor can you ever say, with any propriety, that this act of his is different from that other, or that this judgement or idea has been lately formed, and will give place, by succession, to any different judgement or idea.

I can readily allow, said *Cleanthes*, that those who maintain the perfect simplicity of the supreme being, to the extent in which you have explained it, are complete *mystics*, and chargeable with all the consequences which I have drawn from their opinion. They are, in a word, atheists, without knowing it. For though it be allowed, that the deity possesses attributes, of which we have no comprehension; yet ought we never to ascribe to him any attributes, which are absolutely incompatible with that intelligent nature, essential to him. A mind, whose acts and sentiments and ideas are not distinct and successive; one, that is wholly simple, and totally immutable; is a mind, which has no thought, no reason, no will, no sentiment, no love, no hatred; or in a word, is no mind at all. It is an abuse of terms to give it that appellation;

and we may as well speak of limited extension without figure, or of number without composition.

Pray consider, said *Philo*, whom you are at present inveighing against. You are honouring with the appellation of atheist all the sound, orthodox divines almost, who have treated of this subject; and you will, at last be, yourself, found, according to your reckoning, the only sound theist in the world. But if idolators be atheists, as, I think, may justly be asserted, and Christian theologians the same; what becomes of the argument, so much celebrated, derived from the universal consent of mankind?[34]

But because I know you are not much swayed by names and authorities, I shall endeavour to show you, a little more distinctly, the inconveniences of that anthropomorphism, which you have embraced; and shall prove, that there is no ground to suppose a plan of the world to be formed in the divine mind, consisting of distinct ideas, differently arranged; in the same manner as an architect forms in his head the plan of a house which he intends to execute.

It is not easy, I own, to see, what is gained by this supposition, whether we judge of the matter by *reason* or by *experience*. We are still obliged to mount higher, in order to find the cause of this cause, which you had assigned as satisfactory and conclusive.

If *reason* (I mean abstract reason, derived from enquiries *a priori*) be not alike mute with regard to all questions concerning cause and effect; this sentence at least it will venture to pronounce, that a mental world or universe of ideas requires a cause as much as does a material world or universe of objects; and if similar in its arrangement must require a similar cause. For what is there in this subject, which should occasion a different conclusion or inference? In an abstract view, they are entirely alike; and no difficulty attends the one supposition, which is not common to both of them.

Again, when we will needs force *experience* to pronounce some sentence, even on these subjects, which lie beyond her sphere; neither can she perceive any material difference in this particular, between these two kinds of worlds, but finds them to be governed by similar principles, and to depend upon an equal variety of causes in their operations. We have specimens in miniature of both of them. Our own mind resembles the one: A vegetable or animal body the other. Let experience, therefore, judge from these samples. Nothing seems more delicate with regard to its causes than thought; and as these causes never operate in two persons after the same manner, so we never find two persons, who think exactly alike. Nor indeed does the same person think exactly alike at any two different periods of time. A difference of age, of the disposition of his body, of weather, of food, of company, of books, of passions; any of these particulars or others more minute, are sufficient to alter the curious machinery of thought, and communicate to it very different movements and operations. As far as we can judge, vegetables and animal bodies are not more delicate in their motions, nor depend upon a greater variety or more curious adjustment of springs and principles.

How therefore shall we satisfy ourselves concerning the cause of that being, whom you suppose the author of nature, or, according to your system of anthropomorphism, the ideal world, into which you trace the material? Have we not the same reason to trace that ideal world into another ideal world, or new intelligent principle? But if we stop, and go no farther; why go so far? Why not stop at the material world? How can we satisfy ourselves without going on *in infinitum*? And after all, what satisfaction is there in that infinite progression? Let us remember the story of the Indian philosopher and his elephant.[35] It was never more applicable than to the present subject. If the material world rests upon a similar ideal world, this ideal world must rest upon some other; and so on, without end. It were better, therefore, never to look beyond the present material world. By supposing it to contain the principle of its order within itself, we really assert it to be God; and the sooner we arrive at that divine being, so much the better. When you go one step beyond the mundane system, you only excite an inquisitive humour, which it is impossible ever to satisfy.

To say, that the different ideas, which compose the reason of the supreme being, fall into order, of themselves, and by their own nature, is really to talk without any precise meaning. If it has a meaning, I would fain know, why it is not as good sense to say, that the parts of the material world fall into order, of themselves, and by their own nature? Can the one opinion be intelligible, while the other is not so?

We have, indeed, experience of ideas, which fall into order, of themselves, and without any *known* cause: But, I am sure, we have a much larger experience of matter, which does the same; as in all instances of generation and vegetation, where the accurate analysis of the cause exceeds all human comprehension. We have also experience of particular systems of thought and of matter, which have no order; of the first, in madness, of the second, in corruption. Why then should we think, that order is more essential to one than the other? And if it requires a cause in both, what do we gain by your system, in tracing the universe of objects into a similar universe of ideas? The first step, which we make, leads us on for ever. It were, therefore, wise in us to limit all our inquiries to the present world, without looking farther. No satisfaction can ever be attained by these speculations, which so far exceed the narrow bounds of human understanding.

It was usual with the *Peripatetics*, you know, *Cleanthes*, when the cause of any phenomenon was demanded, to have recourse to their *faculties* or *occult qualities*, and to say, for instance, that bread nourished by its nutritive faculty, and senna purged by its purgative: But it has been discovered, that this subterfuge was nothing but the disguise of ignorance; and that these philosophers, though less ingenuous, really said the same thing with the sceptics or the vulgar, who fairly confessed, that they knew not the cause of these phenomena. In like manner, when it is asked, what cause produces order in the ideas of the supreme being, can any other reason be assigned by you anthropomorphites, than that it is a *rational* faculty, and that such is the nature of the deity? But why a similar answer will not be equally satisfactory in accounting for the order of the world, without having recourse to any such intelligent creator, as you insist on, may be difficult to determine. It is only to say, that *such* is the nature of material objects, and that they are all originally possessed of a *faculty* of order and proportion. These are only more learned and elaborate ways of confessing our ignorance; nor has the one hypothesis any real advantage above the other, except in its greater conformity to vulgar prejudices.

You have displayed this argument with great emphasis, replied *Cleanthes*: You seem not sensible, how easy it is to answer it. Even in common life, if I assign a cause for any event; is it any objection, *Philo*, that I cannot assign the cause of that cause, and answer every new question, which may incessantly be started? And what philosophers could possibly submit to so rigid a rule? Philosophers, who confess ultimate causes to be totally unknown, and are sensible, that the most refined principles, into which they trace the phenomena, are still to them as inexplicable as these phenomena themselves are to the vulgar. The order and arrangement of nature, the curious adjustment of final causes, the plain use and intention of every part and organ; all these bespeak in the clearest language an intelligent cause or author. The heavens and the earth join in the same testimony: The whole chorus of nature raises one hymn to the praises of its creator:[36] You alone, or almost alone, disturb this general harmony. You start abstruse doubts, cavils, and objections: You ask me, what is the cause of this cause? I know not; I care not; That concerns not me. I have found a deity; and here I stop my inquiry. Let those go farther, who are wiser or more enterprising.

I pretend to be neither, replied *Philo*: And for that very reason, I should never perhaps have attempted to go so far; especially when I am sensible, that I must at last be contented to sit down with the same answer, which, without farther trouble, might have satisfied me from the beginning. If I am still to remain in utter ignorance of causes, and can absolutely give an explication of nothing, I shall never esteem it any advantage to shove off for a moment a difficulty, which, you acknowledge, must immediately, in its full force, recur upon me. Naturalists indeed very justly explain particular effects by more general causes; though these general causes themselves should remain in the end totally inexplicable: But they never surely thought it satisfactory to explain a particular effect by a particular cause, which was no more to be accounted for than the effect itself. An ideal system, arranged of itself, without a precedent design, is not a whit more explicable than a material one, which attains its order in a like manner; nor is there any more difficulty in the latter supposition than in the former.

PART V

BUT to show you still more inconveniences, continued *Philo*, in your anthropomorphism; please to take a new survey of your principles. *Like effects prove like causes.* This is the experimental argument; and this, you say too, is the sole theological argument. Now it is certain, that the liker the effects are, which are seen, and the liker the causes, which are inferred, the stronger is the argument. Every departure on either side diminishes the probability, and renders the experiment less conclusive. You cannot doubt of the principle: Neither ought you reject its consequences.

All the new discoveries in astronomy, which prove the immense grandeur and magnificence of the works of nature, are so many additional arguments for a deity, according to the true system of theism: But according to your hypothesis of experimental theism they become so many objections, by removing the effect still farther from all resemblance to the effects of human art and contrivance. For if *Lucretius*,* even following the old system of the world, could exclaim:

> Quis regere immensi summam; quis habere profundi
> Indu manu validas potis est moderanter habenas?
> Quis pariter coelos omnes convertere? et omnes
> Ignibus aetheriis terras suffire feraces?
> Omnibus inque locis esse omni tempore praesto?

If *Tully*† esteemed this reasoning so natural as to put it into the mouth of his *Epicurean. Quibus enim oculis animi intueri potuit*

* Lib. II. 1094[37]
† De. nat. Deor. Lib. 1.[38]

vester **Plato** *fabricam illam tanti operis, qua construi a deo atque aedificare mundum facit? quae molitio? quae ferramenta? qui vectes? quae machinae? qui ministri tanti muneris fuerunt? quemadmodum autem obedire et parere voluntati architecti aer, ignis, aqua, terra potuerunt?* If this argument, I say, had any force in former ages; how much greater must it have at present; when the bounds of nature are so infinitely enlarged, and such a magnificent scene is opened to us? It is still more unreasonable to form our idea of so unlimited a cause from our experience of the narrow productions of human design and invention.

The discoveries by microscopes, as they open a new universe in miniature, are still objections, according to you; arguments, according to me. The farther we push our researches of this kind, we are still led to infer the universal cause of all to be vastly different from mankind, or from any object of human experience and observation.

And what say you to the discoveries in anatomy, chemistry, botany? ... These surely are no objections, replied *Cleanthes*: They only discover new instances of art and contrivance.[39] It is still the image of mind reflected on us from innumerable objects. Add, a mind *like the human,* said *Philo*. I know of no other, replied *Cleanthes*. And the liker, the better, insisted *Philo*. To be sure, said *Cleanthes*.

Now, *Cleanthes*, said *Philo*, with an air of alacrity and triumph, mark the consequences.[40] *First*. By this method of reasoning, you renounce all claim to infinity in any of the attributes of the deity. For as the cause ought only to be proportioned to the effect, and the effect, so far as it falls under our cognizance, is not infinite; What pretensions have we, upon your suppositions, to ascribe that attribute to the divine being? You will still insist, that, by removing him so much from all similarity to human creatures, we give into the most arbitrary hypothesis, and at the same time, weaken all proofs of his existence.

Secondly. You have no reason, on your theory, for ascribing perfection to the deity, even in his finite capacity; or for supposing him free from every error, mistake, or incoherence, in his undertakings. There are many inexplicable difficulties in the works of nature, which, if we allow a perfect author to be proved *a priori*, are easily solved, and become only seeming difficulties from the narrow capacity of man, who cannot trace infinite relations.[41] But according to your method of reasoning, these difficulties become all real; and perhaps will be insisted on, as new instances of likeness to human art and contrivance. At least, you must acknowledge, that it is impossible for us to tell, from our limited views, whether this system contains any great faults, or deserves any considerable praise, if compared to other possible, and even real systems. Could a peasant, if the *Aeneid* were read to him, pronounce that poem to be absolutely faultless, or even assign it to its proper rank among the productions of human wit; he, who had never seen any other production?

But were this world ever so perfect a production, it must still remain uncertain, whether all the excellences of the work can justly be ascribed to the workman. If we survey a ship, what an exalted idea must we form of the ingenuity of the carpenter, who framed so complicated useful and beautiful a machine? And what surprise must we entertain, when we find him a stupid mechanic, who imitated others, and copied an art, which, through a long succession of ages, after multiplied trials, mistakes, corrections, deliberations, and controversies, had been gradually improving? Many worlds might have been botched and bungled, throughout an eternity, ere this system was struck out: Much labour lost: Many fruitless trials made: And a slow, but continued improvement carried on during infinite ages in the art of world-making. In such subjects, who can determine, where the truth; nay, who can conjecture where the probability, lies; amidst a great number of hypotheses, which may be proposed, and a still greater number, which may be imagined?

And what shadow of an argument, continued *Philo*, can you produce from your hypothesis, to prove the unity of the deity? A great number of men join in building a house or ship, in rearing a city, in framing a commonwealth: Why may not several deities combine in contriving and framing a world? This is only so much greater similarity to human affairs. By sharing the work among several, we may so much farther limit the attributes of each, and get rid of that extensive power and knowledge, which must be supposed in one deity, and which, according to you, can only serve to weaken the proof of his existence. And if such foolish, such vicious creatures as man can yet often unite in framing and executing one plan, how much more those deities or demons, whom we may suppose several degrees more perfect?

To multiply causes without necessity is indeed contrary to true philosophy: But this principle applies not to the present case. Were one deity antecedently proved by your theory, who were possessed of every attribute, requisite to the production of the universe; it would be needless, I own (though not absurd) to suppose any other deity existent. But while it is still a question, whether all these attributes are united in one subject, or dispersed among several independent beings: By what phenomena in nature can we pretend to decide the controversy? Where we see a body raised in a scale, we are sure that there is in the opposite scale, however concealed from sight, some counterpoising weight equal to it: But it is still allowed to doubt, whether that weight be an aggregate of several distinct bodies, or one uniform united mass. And if the weight requisite very much exceeds anything which we have ever seen conjoined in any single body; the former supposition becomes still more probable and natural. An intelligent being of such vast power and capacity, as is necessary to produce the universe, or to speak in the language of ancient philosophy, so prodigious an animal, exceeds all analogy and even comprehension.

But farther, *Cleanthes*; men are mortal, and renew their species by generation; and this is common to all living creatures. The two great sexes of male and female, says *Milton*, animate the world.[42] Why must this circumstance, so universal, so essential, be excluded from those numerous and limited deities? Behold, then, the theogeny of ancient times brought back upon us.

And why not become a perfect anthropomorphite? Why not assert the deity or deities to be corporeal, and to have eyes, a nose, mouth, ears, etc. *Epicurus* maintained, that no man had ever seen reason but in a human figure; therefore, the gods must have a human figure.[43] And this argument, which is deservedly so much ridiculed by *Cicero*, becomes, according to you, solid and philosophical.

In a word, *Cleanthes*, a man, who follows your hypothesis, is able, perhaps, to assert, or conjecture, that the universe, some time, arose from some thing like design: But beyond that position he cannot ascertain one single circumstance, and is left afterwards to fix every point of his theology, by the utmost licence of fancy and hypothesis. This world, for aught he knows, is very faulty and imperfect, compared to a superior standard; and was only the first rude essay of some infant deity, who afterwards abandoned it, ashamed of his lame performance: It is the work only of some dependent, inferior deity; and is the object of derision to his superiors: It is the production of old age and dotage in some superannuated deity; and ever since his death, has run on at adventures, from the first impulse and active force, which it received from him . . . You justly give signs of horror, *Demea*, at these strange suppositions: But these, and a thousand more of the same kind, are *Cleanthes'* suppositions, not mine. From the moment the attributes of the deity are supposed finite, all these have a place. And I cannot, for my part, think, that so wild and unsettled a system of theology is, in any respect, preferable to none at all.

These suppositions I absolutely disown; cried *Cleanthes*: They strike me, however, with no horror; especially, when proposed in that rambling way, in which they drop from you. On the contrary, they give me pleasure, when I see, that, by the utmost indulgence of your imagination, you never get rid of the hypothesis of design in the universe; but are obliged, at every turn, to have recourse to it. To this concession I adhere steadily; and this I regard as a sufficient foundation for religion.

PART VI

IT must be a slight fabric, indeed, said *Demea*, which can be erected on so tottering a foundation. While we are uncertain, whether there is one deity or many; whether the deity or deities, to whom we owe our existence, be perfect or imperfect, subordinate or supreme, dead or alive; what trust or confidence can we repose in them? What devotion or worship address to them? What veneration or obedience pay them? To all the purposes of life, the theory of religion becomes altogether useless; and even with regard to speculative consequences, its uncertainty, according to you, must render it totally precarious and unsatisfactory.

To render it still more unsatisfactory, said *Philo*, there occurs to me another hypothesis, which must acquire an air of probability from the method of reasoning so much insisted upon by *Cleanthes*. That like effects arise from like causes: This principle he supposes the foundation of all religion. But there is another principle of the same kind, no less certain, and derived from the same source of experience; that where several known circumstances are *observed* to be similar, the unknown will also be *found* similar. Thus, if we see the limbs of a human body, we conclude that it is also attended with a human head, though hid from us. Thus, if we see, through a chink in a wall, a small part of the sun, we conclude that, were the wall removed, we should see the whole body. In short, this method of reasoning is so obvious and familiar, that no scruple can ever be made with regard to its solidity.

Now if we survey the universe, so far as it falls under our knowledge, it bears a great resemblance to an animal or organized body, and seems actuated with a like principle of life and motion.

A continual circulation of matter in it produces no disorder: A continual waste in every part is incessantly repaired: The closest sympathy is perceived throughout the entire system: And each part or member, in performing its proper offices, operates both to its own preservation and to that of the whole. The world, therefore, I infer, is an animal, and the deity is the SOUL of the world, actuating it, and actuated by it.

You have too much learning, *Cleanthes*, to be at all surprised at this opinion, which, you know, was maintained by almost all the theists of antiquity, and chiefly prevails in their discourses and reasonings.[44] For though sometimes the ancient philosophers reason from final causes, as if they thought the world the workmanship of God; yet it appears rather their favourite notion to consider it as his body, whose organization renders it subservient to him. And it must be confessed, that as the universe resembles more a human body than it does the works of human art and contrivance; if our limited analogy could ever, with any propriety, be extended to the whole of nature, the inference seems juster in favour of the ancient than the modern theory.

There are many other advantages too, in the former theory, which recommended it to the ancient theologians. Nothing more repugnant to all their notions, because nothing more repugnant to common experience, than mind without body; a mere spiritual substance, which fell not under their senses nor comprehension, and of which they had not observed one single instance throughout all nature. Mind and body they knew, because they felt both: And order, arrangement, organization, or internal machinery in both they likewise knew, after the same manner: And it could not but seem reasonable to transfer this experience to the universe, and to suppose the divine mind and body to be also coeval, and to have, both of them, order and arrangement naturally inherent in them, and inseparable from them.

Here, therefore, is a new species of anthropomorphism, *Cleanthes*, on which you may deliberate; and a theory, which seems not liable to any considerable difficulties. You are too much superior surely to *systematical prejudices*, to find any more difficulty in supposing an animal body to be, originally, of itself or from unknown causes, possessed of order and organization, than in supposing a similar order to belong to mind. But the *vulgar prejudice*, that body and mind ought always to accompany each other, ought not, one should think, to be entirely neglected; since it is founded on *vulgar experience*, the only guide which you profess to follow in all these theological inquiries. And if you assert, that our limited experience is an unequal standard, by which to judge of the unlimited extent of nature; you entirely abandon your own hypothesis, and must thenceforward adopt our mysticism, as you call it, and admit of the absolute incomprehensibility of the divine nature.

This theory, I own, replied *Cleanthes*, has never before occurred to me, though a pretty natural one; and I cannot readily, upon so short an examination and reflection, deliver any opinion with regard to it. You are very scrupulous, indeed, said *Philo*; Were I to examine any system of yours, I should not have acted with half that caution and reserve, in starting objections and difficulties to it. However, if anything occur to you, you will oblige us by proposing it.

Why then, replied *Cleanthes*, it seems to me, that, though the world does, in many circumstances, resemble an animal body, yet is the analogy also defective in many circumstances, the most material: No organs of sense; no seat of thought or reason; no one precise origin of motion and action. In short, it seems to bear a stronger resemblance to a vegetable than to an animal; and your inference would be so far inconclusive in favour of the soul of the world.

But in the next place, your theory seems to imply the eternity of the world; and that is a principle, which, I think, can be refuted by the strongest reasons and probabilities. I shall suggest an argument to this purpose, which, I believe, has not been insisted on by any writer. Those, who reason from the late origin of arts and sciences, though their inference wants not force, may perhaps be refuted by considerations, derived from the nature of human society, which is in continual revolution, between ignorance and knowledge, liberty and slavery, riches and poverty; so that it is impossible for us, from our limited experience, to foretell with assurance what events may or may not be expected. Ancient learning and history seem to have been in great danger of entirely perishing after the inundation of the barbarous nations; and had these convulsions continued a little longer or been a little more violent, we should not probably have now known what passed in the world a few centuries before us. Nay, were it not for the superstition of the popes, who preserved a little jargon of Latin in order to support the appearance of an ancient and universal church, that tongue must have been utterly lost: In which case the western world, being totally barbarous, would not have been in a fit disposition for receiving the Greek language and learning, which was conveyed to them after the sacking of Constantinople. When learning and books had been extinguished, even the mechanical arts would have fallen considerably to decay; and it is easily imagined, that fable or tradition might ascribe to them a much later origin than the true one. This vulgar argument, therefore, against the eternity of the world, seems a little precarious.

But here appears to be the foundation of a better argument. Lucullus[45] was the first that brought cherry trees from Asia to Europe; though that tree thrives so well in many European climates, that it grows in the woods without any culture. Is it possible, that throughout a whole eternity, no European had ever passed into Asia, and thought of transplanting so delicious a fruit into his own country? Or if the tree was once transplanted and propagated, how could it ever afterwards perish? Empires may rise and fall; liberty and slavery succeed alternately; ignorance and knowledge give place to each other; but the cherry tree will still remain in the woods of Greece, Spain and Italy, and will never be affected by the revolutions of human society.

It is not two thousand years, since vines were transplanted into France; though there is no climate in the world more favourable to them. It is not three centuries since horses, cows, sheep, swine, dogs, corn were known in America. Is it possible, that, during the revolutions of a whole eternity, there never arose a *Columbus*, who might open the communication between Europe and that continent? We may as well imagine, that all men would wear stockings for ten thousand years, and never have the sense to think of garters to tie them. All these seem convincing proofs of the youth, or rather infancy of the world; as being founded on the operation of principles more constant and steady, than those by which human society is governed and directed. Nothing less than a total convulsion of the elements will ever destroy all the European animals and vegetables, which are now to be found in the Western world.

And what argument have you against such convulsions? replied *Philo*. Strong and almost incontestable proofs may be traced over the whole earth that every part of this globe has continued for many ages entirely covered with water. And though order were supposed inseparable from matter, and inherent in it; yet may matter be susceptible of many and great revolutions, through the endless periods of eternal duration. The incessant changes, to which every part of it is subject, seem to intimate some such general transformations; though at the same time, it is observable, that all the changes, and corruptions, of which we have ever had experience, are but passages from one state of order to another; nor can matter ever rest in total deformity and confusion. What we see in the parts, we may infer in the whole; at least, that is the method of reasoning, on which you rest your whole theory. And were I obliged to defend any particular system of this nature (which I never willingly should do) I esteem none more plausible, than that which ascribes an eternal, inherent principle of order to the world; though attended with great and continual revolutions and alterations. This at once solves all difficulties; and if the solution, by being so general, is not entirely complete and satisfactory, it is, at least, a theory, that we must, sooner or later, have recourse to, whatever system we embrace. How could things have been as they are, were there not an original inherent principle of order somewhere, in thought or in matter? And it is very indifferent to which of these we give the preference. Chance has no place, on any hypothesis, sceptical or religious. Everything is surely governed by steady, inviolable laws.[46] And were the inmost essence of things laid open to us, we should then discover a scene, of which, at present, we can have no idea. Instead of admiring the order of natural beings, we should clearly see that it was absolutely impossible for them, in the smallest article, ever to admit of any other disposition.

Were anyone inclined to revive the ancient pagan theology, which maintained, as we learn from *Hesiod*,[47] that this globe was governed by 30,000 deities, who arose from the unknown powers of nature: You would naturally object, *Cleanthes*, that nothing is gained by this hypothesis, and that it is as easy to suppose all men and animals, being more numerous, but less perfect, to have sprung immediately from a like origin. Push the same inference a step further; and you will find a numerous society of deities as explicable as one universal deity, who possesses, within himself, the powers and perfections of the whole society. All these systems, then, of scepticism, polytheism, and theism you must allow, on your principles, to be on a like footing, and that no one of them has any advantages over the others. You may thence learn the fallacy of your principles.

PART VII

BUT here, continued *Philo*, in examining the ancient system of the soul of the world, there strikes me, all on a sudden, a new idea, which, if just, must go near to subvert all your reasoning, and destroy even your first inferences, on which you repose such confidence. If the universe bears a greater likeness to animal bodies and to vegetables, than to the works of human art, it is more probable, that its cause resembles the cause of the former than that of the latter, and its origin ought rather to be ascribed to generation or vegetation than to reason or design. Your conclusion, even according to your own principles, is therefore lame and defective.

Pray open up this argument a little farther, said *Demea*. For I do not rightly apprehend it, in that concise manner, in which you have expressed it.

Our friend, *Cleanthes*, replied *Philo*, as you have heard, asserts, that since no question of fact can be proved otherwise than by experience, the existence of a deity admits not of proof from any other medium. The world, says he, resembles the works of human contrivance: Therefore its cause must also resemble that of the other. Here we may remark, that the operation of one very small part of nature, to wit man, upon another very small part, to wit, that inanimate matter lying within his reach, is the rule, by which *Cleanthes* judges of the origin of the whole; and he measures objects, so widely disproportioned, by the same individual standard. But to waive all objections, drawn from this topic; I affirm, that there are other parts of the universe (besides the machines of human invention) which bear still a greater resemblance to the fabric of the world, and which therefore afford a better conjecture concerning the universal origin of this system. These parts are animals and vegetables. The world plainly resembles more an animal or a vegetable than it does a watch or a knitting loom. Its cause, therefore, it is more probable, resembles the cause of the former. The cause of the former is generation or vegetation. The cause therefore of the world, we may infer to be something similar or analogous to generation or vegetation.

But how is it conceivable, said *Demea*, that the world can arise from anything similar to vegetation or generation?

Very easily, replied *Philo*. In like manner as a tree sheds its seed into the neighbouring fields, and produces other trees; so the great vegetable, the world, or this planetary system, produces within itself certain seeds, which, being scattered into the surrounding chaos, vegetate into new worlds. A comet, for instance, is the seed of a world; and after it has been fully ripened, by passing from sun to sun, and star to star, it is at last tossed into the unformed elements, which everywhere surround this universe, and immediately sprouts up into a new system.

Or if, for the sake of variety (for I see no other advantage) we should suppose this world to be an animal; a comet is the egg of this animal; and in like manner as an ostrich lays its egg in the sand, which, without any further care, hatches the egg and produces a new animal; so . . .

I understand you, says *Demea*: But what wild, arbitrary suppositions are these? What *data* have you for such extraordinary conclusions? And is the slight, imaginary resemblance of the world to a vegetable or an animal sufficient to establish the same inference with regard to both? Objects, which are in general so widely different; ought they to be a standard for each other?

Right, cries *Philo*: This is the topic on which I have all along insisted. I have still asserted, that we have no *data* to establish any system of cosmogony. Our experience, so imperfect in itself, and so limited both in extent and duration, can afford us no probable conjecture concerning the whole of things. But if we must needs fix on some hypothesis; by what rule, pray, ought we to determine our choice? Is there any other rule than the great similarity of the objects compared? And does not a plant or an animal, which springs from vegetation or generation, bear a stronger resemblance to the world, than does any artificial machine, which arises from reason and design?

But what is this vegetation and generation, of which you talk? said *Demea*. Can you explain their operations, and anatomize that fine internal structure, on which they depend?

As much, at least, replied *Philo*, as *Cleanthes* can explain the operations of reason, or anatomize that internal structure, on which *it* depends. But without any such elaborate disquisitions, when I see an animal, I infer, that it sprang from generation; and that with as great certainty as you conclude a house to have been reared by design. These words, *generation, reason,* mark only certain powers and energies in nature, whose effects are known, but whose essence is incomprehensible;[48] and one of these principles, more than the other, has no privilege for being made a standard to the whole of nature.

In reality, *Demea*, it may reasonably be expected, that the larger the views are which we take of things, the better will they conduct us in our conclusions concerning such extraordinary and such magnificent subjects. In this little corner of the world alone, there are four principles, *reason, instinct, generation, vegetation,* which are similar to each other, and are the causes of similar effects. What a number of other principles may we naturally suppose in the immense extent and variety of the universe, could we travel from planet to planet and from system to system, in order to examine each part of this mighty fabric? Any one of these four principles above mentioned (and a hundred others, which lie open to our conjecture) may afford us a theory, by which to judge of the origin of the world; and it is a palpable and egregious partiality to confine our view entirely to that principle, by which our own minds operate. Were this principle more intelligible on that account, such a partiality might be somewhat excusable: But reason, in its internal fabric and structure, is really as little known to us as instinct or vegetation; and perhaps even that vague, undeterminate word nature to which the vulgar refer everything, is not at the bottom more inexplicable. The effects of these principles are all known to us from experience: But the principles themselves, and their manner of operation are totally unknown: Nor is it less intelligible, or less conformable to experience to say, that the world arose by vegetation, from a seed shed by another world, than to say that it arose from a divine reason or contrivance, according to the sense in which *Cleanthes* understands it.

But methinks, said *Demea*, if the world had a vegetative quality, and could sow the seeds of new worlds into the infinite chaos, this power would be still an additional argument for design in its author. For whence could arise so wonderful a faculty but from design? Or how can order spring from anything which perceives not that order which it bestows?

You need only look around you, replied *Philo*, to satisfy yourself with regard to this question. A tree bestows order and organization on that tree, which springs from it, without knowing the order: An animal, in the same manner, on its offspring: A bird, on its nest: And instances of this kind are even more frequent in the world, than those of order, which arise from reason and contrivance. To say that all this order in animals and vegetables proceeds ultimately from design is begging the question; nor can that great point be ascertained otherwise than by proving *a priori*, both that order is, from its nature, inseparably attached to thought, and that it can never, of itself, or from original unknown principles, belong to matter.

But further, *Demea*; this objection, which you urge, can never be made use of by *Cleanthes*, without renouncing a defence, which he has already made against one of my objections. When I inquired concerning the cause of that supreme reason and intelligence, into which he resolves everything; he told me, that the impossibility of satisfying such inquiries could never be admitted as an objection in any species of philosophy. *We must stop somewhere*, says he; *nor is it ever within the reach of human capacity to explain ultimate causes, or show the last connections of any objects. It is sufficient if the steps, so far as we go, are supported by experience and observation.* Now that vegetation and generation, as well as reason, are experienced to be principles of order in nature, is undeniable. If I rest my system of cosmogony on the former, preferably to the latter, it is at my choice. The matter seems entirely arbitrary. And when *Cleanthes* asks me what is the cause of my great vegetative or generative faculty, I am equally entitled to ask him the cause of his great reasoning principle. These questions we have agreed to forbear on both sides; and it is chiefly his interest on the present occasion to stick to this agreement. Judging by our limited and imperfect experience, generation has some privileges above reason: For we see every day the latter arise from the former, never the former from the latter.

Compare, I beseech you, the consequences on both sides. The world, say I, resembles an animal, therefore it is an animal, therefore it arose from generation. The steps, I confess, are wide; yet there is some small appearance of analogy in each step. The world, says *Cleanthes*, resembles a machine, therefore it is a machine, therefore it arose from design. The steps are here equally wide, and the analogy less striking. And if he pretends to carry on *my* hypothesis a step further, and to infer design or reason from the great principle of generation on which I insist; I may, with better authority, use the same freedom to push further his hypothesis, and infer a divine generation or theogony from his principle of reason. I have at least some faint shadow of experience, which is the utmost, that can ever be attained in the present subject. Reason, in innumerable instances, is observed to arise from the principle of generation, and never arise from any other principle.

Hesiod, and all the ancient mythologists, were so struck with this analogy, that they universally explained the origin of nature from an animal birth, and copulation. *Plato* too, so far as he is intelligible, seems to have adopted some such notion in his *Timaeus*.[49]

The *Brahmins* assert, that the world arose from an infinite spider, who spun this whole complicated mass from his bowels, and annihilates afterwards the whole or any part of it, by absorbing it again, and resolving it into his own essence. Here is a species of cosmogony, which appears to us ridiculous; because a spider is a little contemptible animal, whose operations we are never likely to take for a model of the whole universe. But still here is a new species of analogy, even in our globe. And were there a planet, wholly inhabited by spiders, (which is very possible), this inference would there appear as natural and irrefragable as that which in our planet ascribes the origin of all things to design and intelligence, as explained by *Cleanthes*. Why an orderly system may not be spun from the belly as well as from the brain, it will be difficult for him to give a satisfactory reason.

I must confess, *Philo*, replied *Cleanthes*, that, of all men living, the task which you have undertaken, of raising doubts and objections, suits you best, and seems, in a manner, natural and unavoidable to you. So great is your fertility of invention, that I am not ashamed to acknowledge myself unable, on a sudden, to solve regularly such out-of-the-way difficulties as you incessantly start upon me: Though I clearly see, in general, their fallacy and error. And I question not, but you are yourself, at present, in the same case, and have not the solution so ready as the objection; while you must be sensible, that common sense and reason is entirely against you, and that such whimsies, as you have delivered, may puzzle, but never can convince us.[50]

PART VIII

WHAT you ascribe to the fertility of my invention, replied *Philo*, is entirely owing to the nature of the subject. In subjects, adapted to the narrow compass of human reason, there is commonly but one determination, which carries probability or conviction with it;[51] and to a man of sound judgement,[52] all other suppositions, but that one, appear entirely absurd and chimerical. But in such questions, as the present, a hundred contradictory views may preserve a kind of imperfect analogy; and invention has here full scope to exert itself. Without any great effort of thought, I believe that I could, in an instant, propose other systems of cosmogony, which would have some faint appearance of truth; though it is a thousand, a million to one, if either yours or any one of mine be the true system.[53]

For instance; what if I should receive the old *Epicurean* hypothesis?[54] This is commonly, and I believe, justly, esteemed the most absurd system, that has yet been proposed;[55] yet, I know not, whether, with a few alterations, it might not be brought to bear a faint appearance of probability. Instead of supposing matter infinite, as *Epicurus* did; let us suppose it finite. A finite number of particles is only susceptible of finite transpositions: And it must happen, in an eternal duration, that every possible order or position must be tried an infinite number of times. This world, therefore, with all its events, even the most minute, has before been produced and destroyed, and will again be produced and destroyed, without any bounds and limitations. No one who has a conception of the powers of infinite, in comparison of finite, will ever scruple this determination.

But this supposes, said *Demea*, that matter can acquire motion, without any voluntary agent or first mover.

And where is the difficulty, replied *Philo*, of that supposition? Every event, before experience, is equally difficult and incomprehensible; and every event, after experience, is equally easy and intelligible. Motion, in many instances, from gravity, from elasticity, from electricity, begins in matter, without any known voluntary agent; and to suppose always, in these cases, an unknown voluntary agent is mere hypothesis; and hypothesis attended with no advantages. The beginning of motion in matter itself is as conceivable *a priori* as its communication from mind and intelligence.

Besides; why may not motion have been propagated by impulse through all eternity, and the same stock of it, or nearly the same, be still upheld in the universe? As much as is lost by the composition of motion, as much is gained by its resolution. And whatever the causes are, the fact is certain, that matter is, and always has been in continual agitation, as far as human experience or tradition reaches. There is not probably, at present, in the whole universe, one particle of matter at absolute rest.

And this very consideration too, continued *Philo*, which we have stumbled on in the course of the argument, suggests a new hypothesis of cosmogony, that is not absolutely absurd and improbable. Is there a system, an order, an economy of things, by which matter can preserve that perpetual agitation, which seems essential to it, and yet maintain a constancy in the forms, which it produces? There certainly is such an economy: For this is actually the case with the present world. The continual motion of matter, therefore, in less than infinite transpositions, must produce this economy or order; and by its very nature, that order, when once established, supports itself, for many ages, if not to eternity. But wherever matter is so poised, arranged, and adjusted as to continue in perpetual motion, and yet preserve a constancy in the forms its situation must of necessity have all the same appearance of art and contrivance, which we observe at present. All the parts of each form must have a relation to each other and to the whole: And the whole itself must have a relation to the other parts of the universe, to the element, in which the form subsists; to the materials, with which it repairs its waste and decay; and to every other form, which is hostile or friendly. A defect in any of these particulars destroys the form; and the matter, of which it is composed, is again set loose, and is thrown into irregular motions and fermentations, till it unite itself to some other regular form. If no such form be prepared to receive it, and if there be a great quantity of this corrupted matter in the universe, the universe itself is entirely disordered; whether it be the feeble embryo of a world in its first beginnings, that is thus destroyed, or the rotten carcass of one, languishing in old age and infirmity. In either case, a chaos ensues; till finite, though innumerable revolutions produce at last some forms, whose parts and organs are so adjusted as to support the forms amidst a continued succession of matter.

Suppose, (for we shall endeavour to vary the expression) that matter were thrown into any position, by a blind, unguided force; it is evident that this first position must in all probability be the most confused and most disorderly imaginable, without any resemblance to those works of human contrivance, which, along with a symmetry of parts, discover an adjustment of means to ends and a tendency to self-preservation. If the actuating force cease after this operation, matter must remain forever in disorder, and continue an immense chaos, without any proportion or activity. But suppose, that the actuating force, whatever it be, still continues in matter, this first position will immediately give place to a second, which will likewise in all probability be as disorderly as the first, and so on, through many successions of changes and revolutions. No particular order or position ever continues a moment unaltered. The original force, still remaining in activity, gives a perpetual restlessness to matter. Every possible situation is produced, and instantly destroyed. If a glimpse or dawn of order appears for a moment, it is instantly hurried away and confounded, by that never-ceasing force, which actuates every part of matter.

Thus the universe goes on for many ages in a continued succession of chaos and disorder. But is it not possible that it may settle at last, so as not to lose its motion and active force (for that we have supposed inherent in it) yet so as to preserve a uniformity of appearance, amidst the continual motion and fluctuation of its parts? This we find to be the case with the universe at present. Every individual is perpetually changing, and every part of every individual, and yet the whole remains, in appearance, the same. May we not hope for such a position, or rather be assured of it, from the eternal revolutions of unguided matter, and may not this account for all the appearing wisdom and contrivance, which is in the universe? Let us contemplate the subject a little, and we shall find, that this adjustment, if attained by matter, of a seeming stability in the forms, with a real and perpetual revolution or motion of parts, affords a plausible, if not a true solution of the difficulty.

It is in vain, therefore, to insist upon the uses of the parts in animals or vegetables and their curious adjustment to each other. I would fain know how an animal could subsist, unless its parts were so adjusted? Do we not find, that it immediately perishes whenever this adjustment ceases, and that its matter corrupting tries some new form? It happens, indeed, that the parts of the world are so well adjusted, that some regular form immediately lays claim to this corrupted matter: And if it were not so, could the world subsist? Must it not dissolve as well as the animal, and pass through new positions and situations; till in great, but finite succession, it fall at last into the present or some such order?

It is well, replied *Cleanthes*, you told us, that this hypothesis was suggested on a sudden, in the course of the argument. Had you had leisure to examine it, you would soon have perceived the insuperable objections, to which it is exposed. No form, you say, can subsist, unless it possess those powers and organs, requisite for its subsistence: Some new order or economy must be tried, and so on, without intermission; till at last some order, which can support and maintain itself, is fallen upon. But according to this hypothesis, whence arise the many conveniences and advantages, which men and all animals possess? Two eyes, two ears are not absolutely necessary for the subsistence of the species. Human race might have been propagated and preserved, without horses, dogs, cows, sheep, and those innumerable fruits and products, which serve to our satisfaction and enjoyment. If no camels had been created for the use of man in the sandy deserts of Africa and Arabia, would the world have been dissolved? If no loadstone had been framed to give that wonderful and useful direction to the needle, would human society and the human kind have been immediately extinguished? Though the maxims of nature be in general very frugal, yet instances of this kind are far from being rare; and any one of them is a sufficient proof of design, and of a benevolent design, which gave rise to the order and arrangement of the universe.[56]

At least, you may safely infer, said *Philo*, that the foregoing hypothesis is so far incomplete and imperfect; which I shall not scruple to allow. But can we ever reasonably expect greater success in any attempts of this nature? Or can we ever hope to erect a system of cosmogony, that will be liable to no exceptions, and will contain no circumstance repugnant to our limited and imperfect experience of the analogy of nature? Your theory itself cannot surely pretend to any such advantage; even though you have run into *anthropomorphism*, the better to preserve a conformity to common experience. Let us once more put it to trial. In all instances which we have ever seen, ideas are copied from real objects, and are ectypal, not archetypal, to express myself in learned terms: You reverse this order, and give thought the precedence. In all instances which we have ever seen, thought has no influence upon matter, except where that matter is so conjoined with it, as to have an equal reciprocal influence upon it. No animal can move immediately anything but the members of its own body; and indeed, the equality of action and reaction seems to be an universal law of nature: But your theory implies a contradiction to this experience. These instances, with many more, which it were easy to collect (particularly the supposition of a mind or system of thought that is eternal, or in other words, an animal ingenerable and immortal) these instances, I say, may teach, all of us, sobriety in condemning each other, and let us see, that as no system of this kind ought ever to be received from a slight analogy, so neither ought any to be rejected on account of a small incongruity. For that is an inconvenience, from which we can justly pronounce no one to be exempted.

All religious systems, it is confessed, are subject to great and insuperable difficulties. Each disputant triumphs in his turn; while he carries on an offensive war, and exposes the absurdities, barbarities, and pernicious tenets of his antagonist. But all of them, on the whole, prepare a complete triumph for the sceptic, who tells them, that <u>no system ought ever to be embraced with regard to such subjects: For this plain reason, that no absurdity ought ever to be assented to with regard to any subject. A total suspense of judgement is here our only reasonable resource.</u>[57] And if every attack, as is commonly observed, and no defence, among theologians, is successful; how complete must be *his* victory, who remains always, with all mankind, on the offensive, and has himself no fixed station or abiding city, which he is ever, on any occasion, obliged to defend?

PART IX

BUT if so many difficulties attend the argument *a posteriori*, said *Demea*; had we not better adhere to that simple and sublime argument *a priori*, which, by offering to us infallible demonstration, cuts off at once all doubt and difficulty? By this argument too, we may prove the INFINITY of the divine attributes, which, I am afraid, can never be ascertained with certainty from any other topic.[58] For how can an effect, which either is finite, or, for aught we know, may be so; how can such an effect, I say, prove an infinite cause? The unity too of the divine nature, it is very difficult, if not absolutely impossible, to deduce merely from contemplating the works of nature; nor will the uniformity alone of the plan, even were it allowed, give us any assurance of that attribute. Whereas the argument *a priori* . .

You seem to reason, *Demea*, interposed *Cleanthes*, as if those advantages and conveniences in the abstract argument were full proofs of its solidity. But it is first proper, in my opinion, to determine what argument of this nature you choose to insist on; and we shall afterwards, from itself, better than from its *useful* consequences, endeavour to determine what value we ought to put upon it.

The argument, replied *Demea*, which I would insist on is the common one. Whatever exists must have a cause or reason of its existence; it being absolutely impossible for any thing to produce itself, or be the cause of its own existence. In mounting up, therefore, from effects to causes, we must either go on in tracing an infinite succession, without any ultimate cause at all, or must at last have recourse to some ultimate cause, that is *necessarily* existent: Now that the first supposition is absurd may be thus proved. In the infinite chain or succession of causes and effects, each single effect is determined to exist by the power and efficacy of that cause, which immediately preceded; but the whole eternal chain or succession, taken together, is not determined or caused by any thing: And yet it is evident that it requires a cause or reason, as much as any particular object, which begins to exist in time. The question is still reasonable, why this particular succession of causes existed from eternity, and not any other succession, or no succession at all. If there be no necessarily existent being, any supposition, which can be formed, is equally possible; nor is there any more absurdity in nothing's having existed from eternity, than there is in that succession of causes, which constitutes the universe. What was it then, which determined something to exist rather than nothing, and bestowed being on a particular possibility, exclusive of the rest? *External causes*, there are supposed to be none. *Chance* is a word without meaning. Was it *nothing*? But that can never produce anything. We must, therefore, have recourse to a necessarily existent being who carries the REASON of his existence in himself; and who cannot be supposed not to exist without an express contradiction. There is, consequently, such a being, that is, there is a deity.[59]

I shall not leave it to *Philo*, said *Cleanthes*, (though I know that the starting objections is his chief delight) to point out the weakness of this metaphysical reasoning. It seems to me so obviously ill-grounded, and at the same time of so little consequence to the cause of true piety and religion, that I shall myself venture to show the fallacy of it.

I shall begin with observing, that there is an evident absurdity in pretending to demonstrate a matter of fact, or to prove it by any arguments *a priori*. Nothing is demonstrable unless the contrary implies a contradiction. Nothing that is distinctly conceivable implies a contradiction. Whatever we conceive as existent, we can also conceive as non-existent. There is no being, therefore, whose non-existence implies a contradiction. Consequently there is no being, whose existence is demonstrable. I propose this argument as entirely decisive, and am willing to rest the whole controversy upon it.[60]

It is pretended, that the deity is a necessarily existent being, and this necessity of his existence is attempted to be explained by asserting, that, if we knew his whole essence or nature, we should perceive it to be as impossible for him not to exist as for twice two not to be four. But it is evident, that this can never happen, while our faculties remain the same as at present. It will still be possible for us, at any time, to conceive the non-existence of what we formerly conceived to exist; nor can the mind ever lie under a necessity of supposing any object to remain always in being; in the same manner as we lie under a necessity of always conceiving twice two to be four. The words, therefore, *necessary existence* have no meaning; or which is the same thing, none that is consistent.

But farther; why may not the material universe be the necessarily existent being, according to this pretended explication of necessity? We dare not affirm that we know all the qualities of matter; and for aught we can determine, it may contain some qualities, which, were they known, would make its non-existence appear as great a contradiction as that twice two is five. I find only one argument employed to prove, that the material world is not the necessarily existent being; and this argument is derived from the contingency both of the matter and the form of the world. 'Any particle of matter', it is said,* 'may be *conceived* to be annihilated; and any form may be *conceived* to be altered. Such an annihilation or alteration, therefore, is not impossible'. But it seems a great partiality not to perceive, that the same argument extends equally to the deity, so far as we have any conception of him; and that the mind can at least imagine him to be non-existent, or his attributes to be altered. It must be some unknown, inconceivable qualities, which can make his non-existence appear impossible, or his attributes unalterable: And no reason can be assigned, why these qualities may not belong to matter. As they are altogether unknown and inconceivable, they can never be proved incompatible with it.

Add to this, that in tracing an eternal succession of objects, it

* Dr Clarke[61]

seems absurd to inquire for a general cause or first author. How can any thing that exists from eternity, have a cause; since that relation implies a priority in time and a beginning of existence?[62]

In such a chain too, or succession of objects, each part is caused by that which preceded it, and causes that which succeeds it. Where then is the difficulty? But the WHOLE, you say, wants a cause. I answer, that the uniting of these parts into a whole, like the uniting of several distinct counties into one kingdom, or several distinct members into one body, is performed merely by an arbitrary act of the mind, and has no influence on the nature of things. Did I show you the particular causes of each individual in a collection of twenty particles of matter, I should think it very unreasonable, should you afterwards ask me, what was the cause of the whole twenty. This is sufficiently explained in explaining the cause of the parts.

Though the reasonings, which you have urged, *Cleanthes*, may well excuse me, said *Philo*, from starting any further difficulties; yet I cannot forbear insisting still upon another topic. It is observed by arithmeticians, that the products of 9 compose always either 9 or some lesser product of 9; if you add together all the characters, of which any of the former products is composed. Thus, of 18, 27, 36, which are products of 9, you make 9 by adding 1 to 8, 2 to 7, 3 to 6. Thus 369, is a product also of 9; and if you add 3, 6, and 9, you make 18, a lesser product of 9.* To a superficial observer, so wonderful a regularity may be admired as the effect either of chance or design; but a skilful algebraist immediately concludes it to be the work of necessity, and demonstrates, that it must for ever result from the nature of these numbers. Is it not probable, I ask, that the whole economy of the universe is conducted by a like necessity, though no human algebra can furnish a key, which solves the difficulty? And instead of admiring the order of natural beings, may it not happen, that, could we penetrate into the intimate nature of bodies, we should clearly see why it was absolutely impossible, they could ever admit of any other disposition? So dangerous is it to introduce this idea

* *République des Lettres.* Août 1685.

of necessity into the present question! And so naturally does it afford an inference directly opposite to the religious hypothesis!

But dropping all these abstractions, continued *Philo*, and confining ourselves to more familiar topics; I shall venture to add an observation, that the argument *a priori* has seldom been found very convincing, except to people of a metaphysical head, who have accustomed themselves to abstract reasoning, and who finding from mathematics, that the understanding frequently leads to truth, through obscurity and contrary to first appearances, have transferred the same habit of thinking to subjects, where it ought not to have place. Other people, even of good sense and the best inclined to religion, feel always some deficiency in such arguments, though they are not perhaps able to explain distinctly where it lies. A certain proof, that men ever did, and ever will derive their religion from other sources than this species of reasoning.

PART X

IT is my opinion, I own, replied *Demea*, that each man feels, in a manner, the truth of religion within his own breast; and from a consciousness of his imbecility and misery, rather than from any reasoning, is led to seek protection from that being, on whom he and all nature is dependent. So anxious or so tedious are even the best scenes of life, that futurity is still the object of all our hopes and fears. We incessantly look forward, and endeavour, by prayers, adoration, and sacrifice, to appease those unknown powers, whom we find, by experience, so able to afflict and oppress us. Wretched creatures that we are! What resource for us amidst the innumerable ills of life, did not religion suggest some methods of atonement, and appease those terrors, with which we are incessantly agitated and tormented?

I am indeed persuaded, said *Philo*, that the best and indeed the only method of bringing everyone to a due sense of religion is by just representations of the misery and wickedness of men. And for that purpose a talent of eloquence and strong imagery is more requisite than that of reasoning and argument. For is it necessary to prove, what everyone feels within himself? It is only necessary to make us feel it, if possible, more intimately and sensibly.

The people, indeed, replied *Demea*, are sufficiently convinced of this great and melancholy truth. The miseries of life, the unhappiness of man, the general corruptions of our nature, the unsatisfactory enjoyment of pleasures, riches, honours; these phrases have become almost proverbial in all languages. And who can doubt of what all men declare from their own immediate feeling and experience?

In this point, said *Philo*, the learned are perfectly agreed with the vulgar; and in all letters, *sacred* and *profane*, the topic of human misery has been insisted on with the most pathetic eloquence, that sorrow and melancholy could inspire. The poets, who speak from sentiment, without a system, and whose testimony has therefore the more authority, abound in images of this nature. From *Homer* down to *Dr Young*,[63] the whole inspired tribe have ever been sensible, that no other representation of things would suit the feeling and observation of each individual.

As to authorities, replied *Demea*, you need not seek them. Look round this library of *Cleanthes*. I shall venture to affirm, that, except authors of particular sciences, such as chemistry or botany, who have no occasion to treat of human life, there scarce is one of those innumerable writers, from whom the sense of human misery has not, in some passages or other, extorted a complaint and confession of it. At least, the chance is entirely on that side; and no one author has ever, so far as I can recollect, been so extravagant as to deny it.

There you must excuse me, said *Philo*: *Leibniz* has denied it; and is perhaps the first,* who ventured upon so bold and paradoxical an opinion; at least, the first, who made it essential to his philosophical system.

And by being the first, replied *Demea*, might he not have been sensible of his error? For is this a subject, in which philosophers can propose to make discoveries, especially in so late an age? And can any man hope by a simple denial (for the subject scarcely admits of reasoning) to bear down the united testimony of mankind, founded on sense and consciousness?

And why should man, added he, pretend to an exemption from the lot of all other animals? The whole earth, believe me, *Philo*, is cursed and polluted. A perpetual war is kindled amongst all living creatures. Necessity, hunger, want stimulate the strong and courageous: fear, anxiety, terror agitate the weak and infirm. The first entrance into life gives anguish to the new-born infant and to its wretched parent: Weakness, impotence, distress attend

---

* That sentiment had been maintained by Dr King and some few others before *Leibniz*; though by none of so great a fame as that German philosopher.[64]

each stage of that life: And it is at last finished in agony and horror.

Observe, too, says *Philo*, the curious artifices of nature, in order to embitter the life of every living being. The stronger prey upon the weaker, and keep them in perpetual terror and anxiety. The weaker too, in their turn, often prey upon the stronger, and vex and molest them without relaxation. Consider that innumerable race of insects, which either are bred on the body of each animal, or flying about infix their stings in him. These insects have others still less than themselves, which torment them. And thus on each hand, before and behind, above and below, every animal is surrounded with enemies, which incessantly seek his misery and destruction.

Man alone, said *Demea*, seems to be, in part, an exception to this rule. For by combination in society, he can easily master lions, tigers, and bears, whose greater strength and agility naturally enable them to prey upon him.

On the contrary, it is here chiefly, cried *Philo*, that the uniform and equal maxims of nature are most apparent. Man, it is true, can, by combination, surmount all his *real* enemies, and become master of the whole animal creation: But does he not immediately raise up to himself *imaginary* enemies, the demons of his fancy, who haunt him with superstitious terrors and blast every enjoyment of life? His pleasure, as he imagines, becomes, in their eyes, a crime: His food and repose give them umbrage and offence: His very sleep and dreams furnish new materials to anxious fear: And even death, his refuge from every other ill, presents only the dread of endless and innumerable woes. Nor does the wolf molest more the timid flock, than superstition does the anxious breast of wretched mortals.[65]

Besides, consider, *Demea*: this very society, by which we surmount those wild beasts, our natural enemies; what new enemies does it not raise to us? What woe and misery does it not occasion? Man is the greatest enemy of man. Oppression, injustice, contempt, contumely, violence, sedition, war, calumny, treachery, fraud; by these they mutually torment each other: And they would soon dissolve that society which they had formed, were it not for the dread of still greater ills, which must attend their separation.

But though these external insults, said *Demea*, from animals, from men, from all the elements which assault us, form a frightful catalogue of woes, they are nothing in comparison of those, which arise within ourselves, from the distempered condition of our mind and body. How many lie under the lingering torment of diseases. Hear the pathetic enumeration of the great poet.

> Intestine stone and ulcer, colic pangs,
> Daemoniac frenzy, moping melancholy,
> And moon-struck madness, pining atrophy,
> Marasmus and wide wasting pestilence.
> Dire was the tossing, deep the groans: DESPAIR
> Tended the sick, busiest from couch to couch.
> And over them triumphant DEATH his dart
> Shook, but delayed to strike, though oft invoked
> With vows, as their chief good and final hope.[66]

The disorders of the mind, continued *Demea*, though more secret, are not perhaps less dismal and vexatious. Remorse, shame, anguish, rage, disappointment, anxiety, fear, dejection, despair: who has ever passed through life without cruel inroads from these tormentors? How many have scarcely ever felt any better sensations? Labour and poverty, so abhorred by everyone, are the certain lot of the far greater number: And those few privileged persons, who enjoy ease and opulence, never reach contentment or true felicity. All the goods of life united would not make a very happy man: But all the ills united would make a wretch indeed; and any one of them almost (and who can be free from every one) nay often the absence of one good (and who can possess all) is sufficient to render life ineligible.

Were a stranger to drop, on a sudden, into this world, I would show him, as a specimen of its ills, a hospital full of diseases, a prison crowded with malefactors and debtors, a field of battle strewed with carcasses, a fleet foundering in the ocean, a nation languishing under tyranny, famine, or pestilence.[67] To turn the gay side of life to him, and give him a notion of its pleasures; whither should I conduct him? to a ball, to an opera, to court? He might justly think, that I was only showing him a diversity of distress and sorrow.

There is no evading such striking instances, said *Philo*, but by apologies, which still farther aggravate the charge. Why have all men, I ask, in all ages, complained incessantly of the miseries of life? — They have no just reason, says one: These complaints proceed only from their discontented, repining, anxious disposition — And can there possibly, I reply, be a more certain foundation of misery, than such a wretched temper?

But if they were really as unhappy as they pretend, says my antagonist, why do they remain in life? —

Not satisfied with life, afraid of death.

This is the secret chain, say I, that holds us. We are terrified, not bribed to the continuance of our existence.

It is only a false delicacy, he may insist, which a few refined spirits indulge, and which has spread these complaints among the whole race of mankind — And what is this delicacy, I ask, which you blame? Is it anything but a greater sensibility to all the pleasures and pains of life? And if the man of a delicate, refined temper, by being so much more alive than the rest of the world, is only so much more unhappy; what judgement must we form in general of human life?

Let men remain at rest, says our adversary; and they will be easy. They are willing artificers of their own misery — No! reply I: An anxious languor follows their repose: Disappointment, vexation, trouble, their activity and ambition.

I can observe something like what you mention in some others, replied *Cleanthes*: But I confess, I feel little or nothing of it in myself; and hope that it is not so common as you represent it.

If you feel not human misery yourself, cried *Demea*, I congratulate you on so happy a singularity. Others, seemingly the most prosperous, have not been ashamed to vent their complaints in the most melancholy strains. Let us attend to the great, the fortunate emperor, *Charles* the fifth, when, tired with human grandeur, he resigned all his extensive dominions into the hands of his son. In the last harangue, which he made on that memorable occasion, he publicly avowed, *that the greatest prosperities which he had ever enjoyed, had been mixed with so many adversities, that he might truly say he had never enjoyed any satisfaction or contentment.*[68] But did the retired life, in which he sought for shelter, afford him any greater happiness? If we may credit his son's account, his repentance commenced the very day of his resignation.

Cicero's fortune, from small beginnings, rose to the greatest lustre and renown; yet what pathetic complaints of the ills of life do his familiar letters, as well as his philosophical discourses, contain? And suitably to his own experience, he introduces *Cato*, the great, the fortunate *Cato*, protesting in his old age, that, had he a new life in his offer, he would reject the present.[69]

Ask yourself, ask any of your acquaintance, whether they would live over again the last ten or twenty years of their life. No! But the next twenty, they say, will be better.

> And from the dregs of life, hope to receive
> What the first sprightly running could not give.[70]

Thus at last they find (such is the greatness of human misery; it reconciles even contradictions) that they complain, at once, of the shortness of life, and of its vanity and sorrow.

And is it possible, *Cleanthes*, said *Philo*, that after all these reflections, and infinitely more, which might be suggested, you can still persevere in your anthropomorphism, and assert the moral attributes of the deity, his justice, benevolence, mercy, and rectitude, to be of the same nature with these virtues in human creatures? His power we allow is infinite: Whatever he wills is executed: But neither man nor any other animal is happy: Therefore he does not will their happiness. His wisdom is infinite: He is never mistaken in choosing the means to any end: But the course of nature tends not to human or animal felicity: Therefore it is not established for that purpose. Through the whole compass of human knowledge, there are no inferences more certain and infallible than these. In what respect, then, do his benevolence and mercy resemble the benevolence and mercy of men?

Epicurus's old questions are yet unanswered. Is he willing to prevent evil, but not able? then is he impotent. Is he able, but not

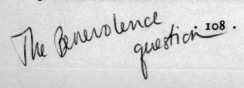

The Benevolence question 108 .

willing? then is he malevolent. Is he both able and willing? whence then is evil?[71]

You ascribe *Cleanthes*, (and I believe justly), a purpose and intention to nature. But what, I beseech you, is the object of that curious artifice and machinery, which she has displayed in all animals? The preservation alone of individuals and propagation of the species. It seems enough for her purpose, if such a rank be barely upheld in the universe, without any care or concern for the happiness of the members that compose it. No resource for this purpose: No machinery, in order merely to give pleasure or ease: No fund of pure joy and contentment: No indulgence without some want or necessity, accompanying it. At least, the few phenomena of this nature are overbalanced by opposite phenomena of still greater importance.

Our sense of music, harmony, and indeed beauty of all kinds gives satisfaction, without being absolutely necessary to the preservation and propagation of the species. But what racking pains, on the other hand, arise from gouts, gravels, megrims, toothaches, rheumatisms, where the injury to the animal-machinery is either small or incurable? Mirth, laughter, play, frolic seem gratuitous satisfactions, which have no further tendency: Spleen, melancholy, discontent, superstition are pains of the same nature. How then does the divine benevolence display itself, in the sense of you anthropomorphites? None but we mystics, as you were pleased to call us, can account for this strange mixture of phenomena, by deriving it from attributes, infinitely perfect, but incomprehensible.[72]

And have you, at last, said *Cleanthes* smiling, betrayed your intentions, *Philo*? Your long agreement with *Demea* did indeed a little surprise me; but I find you were all the while erecting a concealed battery against me. And I must confess, that you have now fallen upon a subject, worthy of your noble spirit of opposition and controversy. If you can make out the present point, and prove mankind to be unhappy or corrupted, there is an end at once of all religion. For to what purpose establish the natural attributes of the deity, while the moral are still doubtful and uncertain?

You take umbrage very easily, replied *Demea*, at opinions the most innocent, and the most generally received even amongst the religious and devout themselves: And nothing can be more surprising than to find a topic like this, concerning the wickedness and misery of man, charged with no less than atheism and profaneness. Have not all pious divines and preachers, who have indulged their rhetoric on so fertile a subject; have they not easily, I say, given a solution of any difficulties, which may attend it? This world is but a point in comparison of the universe: This life but a moment in comparison of eternity. The present evil phenomena, therefore, are rectified in other regions, and in some future period of existence. And the eyes of men, being then opened to larger views of things, see the whole connection of general laws, and trace, with adoration, the benevolence and rectitude of the deity, through all the mazes and intricacies of his providence.

No! replied *Cleanthes*, No! These arbitrary suppositions can never be admitted contrary to matter of fact, visible and uncontroverted. Whence can any cause be known but from its known effects? Whence can any hypothesis be proved but from the apparent phenomena? To establish one hypothesis upon another is building entirely in the air; and the utmost we ever attain, by these conjectures and fictions, is to ascertain the bare possibility of our opinion; but never can we, upon such terms, establish its reality.

The only method of supporting divine benevolence (and it is what I willingly embrace) is to deny absolutely the misery and wickedness of man. Your representations are exaggerated: Your melancholy views mostly fictitious: Your inferences contrary to fact and experience. Health is more common than sickness: Pleasure than pain: Happiness than misery. And for one vexation which we meet with, we attain, upon computation, a hundred enjoyments.

Admitting your position, replied *Philo*, which yet is extremely doubtful; you must, at the same time, allow, that, if pain be less frequent than pleasure, it is infinitely more violent and durable. One hour of it is often able to outweigh a day, a week, a month of our common insipid enjoyments: And how many days, weeks, and months are passed by several in the most acute torments?

Pleasure, scarcely in one instance, is ever able to reach ecstasy and rapture: And in no one instance can it continue for any time at its highest pitch and altitude. The spirits evaporate; the nerves relax; the fabric is disordered; and the enjoyment quickly degenerates into fatigue and uneasiness. But pain often, good God, how often! rises to torture and agony; and the longer it continues, it becomes still more genuine agony and torture. Patience is exhausted; courage languishes; melancholy seizes us; and nothing terminates our misery but the removal of its cause, or another event, which is the sole cure of all evil, but which, from our natural folly, we regard with still greater horror and consternation.

But not to insist upon these topics, continued *Philo*, though most obvious, certain, and important; I must use the freedom to admonish you, *Cleanthes*, that you have put this controversy upon a most dangerous issue, and are unawares introducing a total scepticism into the most essential articles of natural and revealed theology. What! no method of fixing a just foundation for religion, unless we allow the happiness of human life, and maintain a continued existence even in this world, with all our present pains, infirmities, vexations, and follies, to be eligible and desirable! But this is contrary to every one's feeling and experience: It is contrary to an authority so established as nothing can subvert: No decisive proofs can ever be produced against this authority; nor is it possible for you to compute, estimate, and compare all the pains and all the pleasures in the lives of all men and of all animals: And thus by your resting the whole system of religion on a point, which, from its very nature, must forever be uncertain, you tacitly confess, that that system is equally uncertain.

But allowing you, what never will be believed; at least, what you never possibly can prove, that animal, or at least, human happiness in this life exceeds its misery; you have yet done nothing: For this is not, by any means, what we expect from infinite power, infinite wisdom, and infinite goodness. Why is there any misery at all in the world? Not by chance, surely. From some cause then. Is it from the intention of the deity? But he is perfectly benevolent. Is it contrary to his intention? But he is almighty. Nothing can shake the solidity of this reasoning, so short, so clear, so decisive; except we assert, that these subjects exceed all human capacity, and that our common measures of truth and falsehood are not applicable to them; a topic, which I have all along insisted on, but which you have, from the beginning, rejected with scorn and indignation.[73]

But I will be contented to retire still from this retrenchment: For I deny that you can ever force me in it: I will allow, that pain or misery in man is *compatible* with infinite power and goodness in the deity, even in your sense of these attributes: What are you advanced by all these concessions? A mere possible compatibility is not sufficient. You must *prove* these pure, unmixed, and uncontrollable attributes from the present mixed and confused phenomena, and from these alone. A hopeful undertaking! Were the phenomena ever so pure and unmixed, yet, being finite, they would be insufficient for that purpose. How much more, where they are also so jarring and discordant? Here, *Cleanthes*, I find myself at ease in my argument. Here I triumph. Formerly, when we argued concerning the natural attributes of intelligence and design, I needed all my sceptical and metaphysical subtlety to elude your grasp. In many views of the universe, and of its parts, particularly the latter, the beauty and fitness of final causes strike us with such irresistible force that all objections appear (what I believe they really are) mere cavils and sophisms; nor can we then imagine how it was ever possible for us to repose any weight on them. But there is no view of human life or of the condition of mankind, from which, without the greatest violence, we can infer the moral attributes, or learn that infinite benevolence, conjoined with infinite power and infinite wisdom, which we must discover by the eyes of faith alone. It is your turn now to tug the labouring oar, and to support your philosophical subtleties against the dictates of plain reason and experience.

argument
against design
analogy's idea of
God's benevolence + morality
"unhappy man!"

PART XI

I SCRUPLE not to allow, said *Cleanthes*, that I have been apt to suspect the frequent repetition of the word, infinite, which we meet with in all theological writers, to savour more of panegyric than of philosophy, and that any purposes of reasoning, and even of religion, would be better served, were we to rest contented with more accurate and more moderate expressions. The terms, *admirable*, *excellent*, *superlatively great*, *wise*, and *holy*; these sufficiently fill the imaginations of men; and anything beyond, besides that it leads into absurdities, has no influence on the affections or sentiments. Thus, in the present subject, if we abandon all human analogy, as seems your intention, *Demea*, I am afraid we abandon all religion and retain no conception of the great object of our adoration. If we preserve human analogy, we must for ever find it impossible to reconcile any mixture of evil in the universe with infinite attributes; much less, can we ever prove the latter from the former. But supposing the author of nature to be finitely perfect, though far exceeding mankind; a satisfactory account may then be given of natural and moral evil, and every untoward phenomenon be explained and adjusted. A less evil may then be chosen, in order to avoid a greater: Inconveniences be submitted to, in order to reach a desirable end: And in a word, benevolence, regulated by wisdom, and limited by necessity, may produce just such a world as the present. You, *Philo*, who are so prompt at starting views, and reflections, and analogies; I would gladly hear, at length, without interruption, your opinion of this new theory; and if it deserves our attention, we may afterwards, at more leisure, reduce it into form.[74]

My sentiments, replied *Philo*, are not worth being made a

mystery of; and therefore, without any ceremony, I shall deliver what occurs to me, with regard to the present subject. It must, I think, be allowed, that, if a very limited intelligence, whom we shall suppose utterly unacquainted with the universe, were assured, that it were the production of a very good, wise, and powerful being, however finite, he would, from his conjectures, form *beforehand* a different notion of it from what we find it to be by experience; nor would he ever imagine, merely from these attributes of the cause of which he is informed, that the effect could be so full of vice and misery and disorder, as it appears in this life. Supposing now, that this person were brought into the world, still assured, that it was the workmanship of such a sublime and benevolent being; he might, perhaps, be surprised at the disappointment; but would never retract his former belief, if founded on any very solid argument; since such a limited intelligence must be sensible of his own blindness and ignorance, and must allow that there may be many solutions of these phenomena, which will for ever escape his comprehension. But supposing, which is the real case with regard to man, that this creature is not antecedently convinced of a supreme intelligence, benevolent, and powerful, but is left to gather such a belief from the appearances of things; this entirely alters the case, nor will he ever find any reason for such a conclusion. He may be fully convinced of the narrow limits of his understanding, but this will not help him in forming an inference concerning the goodness of superior powers, since he must form that inference from what he knows, not from what he is ignorant of. The more you exaggerate his weakness and ignorance; the more diffident you render him, and give him the greater suspicion, that such subjects are beyond the reach of his faculties. You are obliged, therefore, to reason with him merely from the known phenomena, and to drop every arbitrary supposition or conjecture.

Did I show you a house or palace, where there was not one apartment convenient or agreeable; where the windows, doors, fires, passages, stairs, and the whole economy of the building were the source of noise, confusion, fatigue, darkness, and the extremes of heat and cold; you would certainly blame the contrivance, without any farther examination. The architect would in vain display his subtlety, and prove to you, that if this door or that window were altered, greater ills would ensue. What he says, may be strictly true: The alteration of one particular, while the other parts of the building remain, may only augment the inconveniences. But still you would assert in general, that, if the architect had had skill and good intentions, he might have formed such a plan of the whole, and might have adjusted the parts in such a manner, as would have remedied all or most of these inconveniences. His ignorance or even your own ignorance of such a plan, will never convince you of the impossibility of it. If you find many inconveniences and deformities in the building, you will always, without entering into any detail, condemn the architect.

In short, I repeat the question: Is the world, considered in general, and as it appears to us in this life, different from what a man or such a limited being would, *beforehand*, expect from a very powerful, wise, and benevolent deity? It must be strange prejudice to assert the contrary. And from thence I conclude, that, however consistent the world may be, allowing certain suppositions and conjectures, with the idea of such a deity, it can never afford us an inference concerning his existence. The consistency is not absolutely denied, only the inference. Conjectures, especially where infinity is excluded from the divine attributes, may, perhaps, be sufficient to prove a consistency; but can never be foundations for any inference.

There seem to be *four* circumstances, on which depend all, or the greatest part of the ills, that molest sensible creatures; and it is not impossible but all these circumstances may be necessary and unavoidable. We know so little beyond common life, or even of common life, that, with regard to the economy of a universe, there is no conjecture, however wild, which may not be just; nor any one, however plausible, which may not be erroneous. All that belongs to human understanding, in this deep ignorance and obscurity, is to be sceptical, or at least cautious; and not to admit of any hypothesis, whatever; much less, of any which is supported by no appearance of probability. Now this I assert to be the case with regard to all the causes of evil, and the circumstances, on which it depends. None of them appear to human reason, in the least degree, necessary or unavoidable; nor can we suppose them such, without the utmost license of imagination.

The *first* circumstance, which introduces evil, is that contrivance or economy of the animal creation, by which pains, as well as pleasures, are employed to excite all creatures to action, and make them vigilant in the great work of self-preservation. Now pleasure alone, in its various degrees, seems to human understanding sufficient for this purpose. All animals might be constantly in a state of enjoyment; but when urged by any of the necessities of nature, such as thirst, hunger, weariness; instead of pain, they might feel a diminution of pleasure, by which they might be prompted to seek that object, which is necessary to their subsistence. Men pursue pleasure as eagerly as they avoid pain; at least, might have been so constituted. It seems, therefore, plainly possible to carry on the business of life without any pain. Why then is any animal ever rendered susceptible of such a sensation? If animals can be free from it an hour, they might enjoy a perpetual exemption from it; and it required as particular a contrivance of their organs to produce that feeling, as to endow them with sight, hearing, or any of the senses. Shall we conjecture, that such a contrivance was necessary, without any appearance of reason? And shall we build on that conjecture as on the most certain truth?

But a capacity of pain would not alone produce pain, were it not for the *second* circumstance, viz., the conducting of the world by general laws; and this seems no wise necessary to a very perfect being. It is true; if everything were conducted by particular volitions, the course of nature would be perpetually broken, and no man could employ his reason in the conduct of life. But might not other particular volitions remedy this inconvenience? In short, might not the deity exterminate all ill, wherever it were to be found; and produce all good, without any preparation or long progress of causes and effects?

Besides, we must consider, that, according to the present economy of the world, the course of nature, though supposed exactly regular, yet to us appears not so, and many events are uncertain, and many disappoint our expectations. Health and sickness, calm and tempest, with an infinite number of other accidents, whose causes are unknown and variable, have a great influence both on the fortunes of particular persons and on the prosperity of public societies: And indeed all human life, in a manner, depends on such accidents. A being, therefore, who knows the secret springs of the universe, might easily, by particular volitions, turn all these accidents to the good of mankind, and render the whole world happy, without discovering himself in any operation. A fleet, whose purposes were salutary to society, might always meet with a fair wind: Good princes enjoy sound health and long life: Persons, born to power and authority, be framed with good tempers and virtuous dispositions. A few such events as these, regularly and wisely conducted, would change the face of the world; and yet would no more seem to disturb the course of nature or confound human conduct, than the present economy of things, where the causes are secret, and variable, and compounded. Some small touches, given to *Caligula's* brain in his infancy, might have converted him into a *Trajan*: One wave, a little higher than the rest, by burying *Caesar* and his fortune in the bottom of the ocean, might have restored liberty to a considerable part of mankind. There may, for aught we know, be good reasons, why Providence interposes not in this manner; but they are unknown to us: And though the mere supposition, that such reasons exist, may be sufficient to *save* the conclusion concerning the divine attributes, yet surely it can never be sufficient to *establish* that conclusion.

If everything in the universe be conducted by general laws, and if animals be rendered susceptible of pain, it scarcely seems possible but some ill must arise in the various shocks of matter, and the various concurrence and opposition of general laws: But this ill would be very rare, were it not for the *third* circumstance which I proposed to mention, *viz.*, the great frugality, with which all powers and faculties are distributed to every particular being. So well adjusted are the organs and capacities of all animals, and so well fitted to their preservation, that, as far as history or tradition reaches, there appears not to be any single species, which has yet been extinguished in the universe.[75] Every animal has the requisite endowments; but these endowments are bestowed with so scrupulous an economy, that any considerable diminution must entirely destroy the creature. Wherever one power is increased, there is a proportional abatement in the others. Animals, which excel in swiftness are commonly defective in force. Those, which possess both, are either imperfect in some of their senses, or are oppressed with the most craving wants. The human species, whose chief excellence is reason and sagacity, is of all others the most necessitous, and the most deficient in bodily advantages; without clothes, without arms, without food, without lodging, without any convenience of life, except what they owe to their own skill and industry. In short, nature seems to have formed an exact calculation of the necessities of her creatures; and like a *rigid master*, has afforded them little more powers and endowments, than what are strictly sufficient to supply those necessities. An *indulgent parent* would have bestowed a large stock, in order to guard against accidents, and secure the happiness and welfare of the creature, in the most unfortunate concurrence of circumstances. Every course of life would not have been so surrounded with precipices, that the least departure from the true path, by mistake or necessity, must involve us in misery and ruin. Some reserve, some fund would have been provided to ensure happiness; nor would the powers and the necessities have been adjusted with so rigid an economy. The author of nature is inconceivably powerful: His force is supposed great, if not altogether inexhaustible; Nor is there any reason, as far as we can judge, to make him observe this strict frugality in his dealings with his creatures. It would have been better, were his power extremely limited, to have created fewer animals, and to have endowed these with more faculties for their happiness and preservation. A builder is never esteemed prudent, who undertakes a plan, beyond what his stock will enable him to finish.

In order to cure most of the ills of human life, I require not that man should have the wings of the eagle, the swiftness of the stag, the force of the ox, the arms of the lion, the scales of the crocodile or rhinoceros; much less do I demand the sagacity of an angel or cherubim. I am contented to take an increase in one single power or faculty of his soul. Let him be endowed with a greater propensity to industry and labour; a more vigorous spring and activity of mind; a more constant bent to business and application. Let the whole species possess naturally an equal diligence with that which many individuals are able to attain by habit and reflection; and the most beneficial consequences, without any allay of ill, is the immediate and necessary result of this endowment. Almost all the moral, as well as natural evils of human life arise from idleness; and were our species, by the original constitution of their frame, exempt from this vice or infirmity, the perfect cultivation of land, the improvement of arts and manufactures, the exact execution of every office and duty, immediately follow; and men at once may fully reach that state of society which is so imperfectly attained by the best regulated government. But as industry is a power, and the most valuable of any, nature seems determined, suitably to her usual maxims, to bestow it on men with a very sparing hand; and rather to punish him severely for his deficiency in it, than to reward him for his attainments. She has so contrived his frame, that nothing but the most violent necessity can oblige him to labour, and she employs all his other wants to overcome, at least in part, the want of diligence, and to endow him with some share of a faculty, of which she has thought fit naturally to bereave him. Here our demands may be allowed very humble, and therefore the more reasonable. If we required the endowments of superior penetration and judgement, of a more delicate taste of beauty, of a nicer sensibility to benevolence and friendship; we might be told, that we impiously pretend to break the order of nature, that we want to exalt ourselves into a higher rank of being, that the presents which we require, not being suitable to our state and condition, would only be pernicious to us. But it is hard; I dare to repeat it, it is hard, that being placed in a world so full of wants and necessities; where almost every being and element is either our foe or refuses us their assistance; we should also have our own temper to struggle with, and should be deprived of that faculty, which can alone fence against these multiplied evils.

The *fourth* circumstance, whence arises the misery and ill of the universe, is the inaccurate workmanship of all the springs and principles of the great machine of nature. It must be acknowledged, that there are few parts of the universe, which seem not to serve some purpose, and whose removal would not produce a visible defect and disorder in the whole. The parts hang all together; nor can one be touched without affecting the rest, in a greater or less degree. But at the same time, it must be observed, that none of these parts or principles, however useful, are so accurately adjusted, as to keep precisely within those bounds, in which their utility consists; but they are, all of them, apt, on every occasion, to run into the one extreme or the other. One would imagine, that this grand production had not received the last hand of the maker; so little finished is every part, and so coarse are the strokes, with which it is executed. Thus, the winds are requisite to convey the vapours along the surface of the globe, and to assist men in navigation: But how oft, rising up to tempests and hurricanes, do they become pernicious? Rains are necessary to nourish all the plants and animals of the earth: But how often are they defective? how often excessive? Heat is requisite to all life and vegetation; but is not always found in the due proportion. On the mixture and secretion of the humours and juices of the body depend the health and prosperity of the animal: But the parts perform not regularly their proper function. What more useful than all the passions of the mind, ambition, vanity, love, anger? But how oft do they break their bounds, and cause the greatest convulsions in society? There is nothing so advantageous in the universe, but what frequently becomes pernicious, by its excess or defect; nor has nature guarded, with the requisite accuracy, against all disorder or confusion. The irregularity is never, perhaps, so great as to destroy any species; but it is often sufficient to involve the individuals in ruin and misery.

On the concurrence, then, of these *four* circumstances does all, or the greatest part of natural evil depend. Were all living creatures incapable of pain, or were the world administered by particular volitions, evil never could have found access into the universe: And were animals endowed with a large stock of powers and faculties, beyond what strict necessity requires; or were the several springs and principles of the universe so accurately framed as to preserve always the just temperament and medium; there must have been very little ill in comparison of what we feel at present. What then shall we pronounce on this occasion? Shall we say, that these circumstances are not necessary, and that they might easily have been altered in the contrivance of the universe? This decision seems too presumptuous for creatures, so blind and ignorant. Let us be more modest in our conclusions. Let us allow, that, if the goodness of the deity (I mean a goodness like the human) could be established on any tolerable reasons *a priori*, these phenomena, however untoward, would not be sufficient to subvert that principle, but might easily, in some unknown manner, be reconcilable to it. But let us still assert, that as this goodness is not antecedently established, but must be inferred from the phenomena, there can be no grounds for such an inference, while there are so many ills in the universe, and while these ills might so easily have been remedied, as far as human understanding can be allowed to judge on such a subject. I am sceptic enough to allow, that the bad appearances, notwithstanding all my reasonings, may be compatible with such attributes as you suppose: But surely they can never prove these attributes. Such a conclusion cannot result from scepticism; but must arise from the phenomena, and from our confidence in the reasonings, which we deduce from these phenomena.

Look round this universe. What an immense profusion of beings, animated and organized, sensible and active! You admire this prodigious variety and fecundity. But inspect a little more narrowly these living existences, the only beings worth regarding. How hostile and destructive to each other! How insufficient all of them for their own happiness! How contemptible or odious to the spectator! The whole presents nothing but the idea of a blind nature, impregnated by a great vivifying principle, and pouring forth from her lap, without discernment or parental care, her maimed and abortive children!

Here the Manichaean system occurs as a proper hypothesis to solve the difficulty.[76] And no doubt, in some respects, it is very specious, and has more probability than the common hypothesis, by giving a plausible account of the strange mixture of good and ill which appears in this life. But if we consider, on the other hand, the perfect uniformity and agreement of the parts of the universe, we shall not discover in it any marks of the combat of a malevolent with a benevolent being. There is indeed an opposition of pains and pleasures in the feelings of sensible creatures: But are not all the operations of nature carried on by an opposition of principles, of hot and cold, moist and dry, light and heavy? The true conclusion is, that the original source of all things is entirely indifferent to all these principles, and has no more regard to good above ill than to heat above cold, or to drought above moisture, or to light above heavy.

There may *four* hypotheses be framed concerning the first causes of the universe: *that* they are endowed with perfect goodness, *that* they have perfect malice, *that* they are opposite and have both goodness and malice, *that* they have neither goodness nor malice. Mixed phenomena can never prove the two former unmixed principles. And the uniformity and steadiness of general laws seem to oppose the third. The fourth, therefore, seems by far the most probable.

What I have said concerning natural evil will apply to moral, with little or no variation; and we have no more reason to infer, that the rectitude of the supreme being resembles human rectitude than that his benevolence resembles the human. Nay, it will be thought, that we have still greater cause to exclude from him moral sentiments, such as we feel them; since moral evil, in the opinion of many, is much more predominant above moral good than natural evil above natural good.

But even though this should not be allowed, and though the virtue, which is in mankind, should be acknowledged much superior to the vice; yet so long as there is any vice at all in the universe, it will very much puzzle you anthropomorphites, how to account for it. You must assign a cause for it, without having recourse to the first cause. But as every effect must have a cause, and that cause another, you must either carry on the progression *in infinitum*, or rest on that original principle, who is the ultimate cause of all things.[77]

Hold! hold! cried *Demea*: Whither does your imagination

hurry you? I joined in alliance with you, in order to prove the incomprehensible nature of the divine being, and refute the principles of *Cleanthes*, who would measure everything by human rule and standard. But I now find you running into all the topics of the greatest libertines and infidels; and betraying that holy cause, which you seemingly espoused. Are you secretly, then, a more dangerous enemy than *Cleanthes* himself?

And are you so late in perceiving it? replied *Cleanthes*. Believe me, *Demea*; your friend, *Philo*, from the beginning, has been amusing himself at both our expense; and it must be confessed, that the injudicious reasoning of our vulgar theology has given him but too just a handle of ridicule. The total infirmity of human reason, the absolute incomprehensibility of the divine nature, the great and universal misery and still greater wickedness of man; these are strange topics surely to be so fondly cherished by orthodox divines and doctors. In ages of stupidity and ignorance, indeed, these principles may safely be espoused; and perhaps, no views of things are more proper to promote superstition, than such as encourage the blind amazement, the diffidence, and melancholy of mankind. But at present –

Blame not so much, interposed *Philo*, the ignorance of these reverend gentlemen. They know how to change their style with the times. Formerly it was a most popular theological topic to maintain, that human life was vanity and misery, and to exaggerate all the ills and pains, which are incident to men. But of late years, divines, we find, begin to retract this position, and maintain, though still with some hesitation, that there are more goods than evils, more pleasures than pains, even in this life. When religion stood entirely upon temper and education, it was thought proper to encourage melancholy; as, indeed, mankind never have recourse to superior powers so readily as in that disposition. But as men have now learned to form principles, and to draw consequences, it is necessary to change the batteries, and to make use of such arguments as will endure, at least, some scrutiny and examination. This variation is the same (and from the same causes) with that which I formerly remarked with regard to scepticism.

Thus *Philo* continued to the last his spirit of opposition, and his censure of established opinions. But I could observe, that *Demea* did not at all relish the latter part of the discourse; and he took the occasion soon after, on some pretence or other, to leave the company.

PART XII

AFTER *Demea*'s departure, *Cleanthes* and *Philo* continued the conversation, in the following manner. Our friend, I am afraid, said *Cleanthes*, will have little inclination to revive this topic of discourse, while you are in company; and to tell the truth, *Philo*, I should rather wish to reason with either of you apart on a subject, so sublime and interesting. Your spirit of controversy, joined to your abhorrence of vulgar superstition, carries you strange lengths, when engaged in an argument; and there is nothing so sacred and venerable, even in your own eyes, which you spare on that occasion.

I must confess, replied *Philo*, that I am less cautious on the subject of natural religion than on any other; both because I know that I can never, on that head, corrupt the principles of any man of common sense, and because no one, I am confident, in whose eyes I appear a man of common sense will ever mistake my intentions. You, in particular, *Cleanthes*, with whom I live in unreserved intimacy; you are sensible, that, notwithstanding the freedom of my conversation, and my love of singular arguments, no one has a deeper sense of religion impressed on his mind, or pays more profound adoration to the divine being, as he discovers himself to reason, in the inexplicable contrivance and artifice of nature. A purpose, an intention, a design strikes everywhere the most careless, the most stupid thinker; and no man can be so hardened in absurd systems, as at all times to reject it. *That nature does nothing in vain*, is a maxim established in all the Schools, merely from the contemplation of the works of nature, without any religious purpose; and, from a firm conviction of its truth, an anatomist, who had observed a new organ or canal, would never be satisfied, till he had also discovered its use and intention. One great foundation of the *Copernican* system is the maxim, *that* nature acts *by the simplest methods, and chooses the most proper means to any end*; and astronomers often, without thinking of it, lay this strong foundation of piety and religion. The same thing is observable in other parts of philosophy: And thus all the sciences almost lead us insensibly to acknowledge a first intelligent author; and their authority is often so much the greater, as they do not directly profess that intention.[78]

It is with pleasure I hear *Galen* reason concerning the structure of the human body. The anatomy of a man, says he,* discovers above 600 different muscles; and whoever duly considers these, will find, that in each of them, nature must have adjusted at least ten different circumstances, in order to attain the end, which she proposed: proper figure, just magnitude, right disposition of the several ends, upper and lower position of the whole, the due insertion of the several nerves, veins, and arteries: So that in the muscles alone, above 6,000 several views and intentions must have been formed and executed. The bones he calculates to be 284: The distinct purposes, aimed at in the structure of each, above forty. What a prodigious display of artifice, even in these simple and homogeneous parts? But if we consider the skin, ligaments, vessels, glandules, humours, the several limbs and members of the body; how must our astonishment rise upon us, in proportion to the number and intricacy of the parts so artificially adjusted? The further we advance in these researches, we discover new scenes of art and wisdom: But descry still, at a distance, farther scenes beyond our reach; in the fine internal structure of the parts, in the economy of the brain, in the fabric of the seminal vessels. All these artifices are repeated in every different species of animal, with wonderful variety, and with exact propriety, suited to the different intentions of nature, in framing each species. And if the infidelity of *Galen*, even when these natural sciences were still imperfect, could not withstand such striking appearances; to what pitch of pertinacious obstinacy must a philosopher

* *De formatione foetus.*[79]

in this age have attained, who can now doubt of a supreme intelligence?[80]

Could I meet with one of this species (who, I thank God, are very rare) I would ask him: Supposing there were a God, who did not discover himself immediately to our senses; were it possible for him to give stronger proofs of his existence than what appear on the whole face of nature? What indeed could such a divine being do, but copy the present economy of things; render many of his artifices so plain, that no stupidity could mistake them; afford glimpses of still greater artifices, which demonstrate his prodigious superiority above our narrow apprehensions; and conceal altogether a great many from such imperfect creatures? Now according to all rules of just reasoning, every fact must pass for undisputed, when it is supported by all the arguments, which its nature admits of; even though these arguments be not, in themselves, very numerous or forcible: How much more, in the present case, where no human imagination can compute their number, and no understanding estimate their cogency?

I shall further add, said *Cleanthes*, to what you have so well urged, that one great advantage of the principle of theism is, that it is the only system of cosmogony, which can be rendered intelligible and complete, and yet can throughout preserve a strong analogy to what we every day see and experience in the world. The comparison of the universe to a machine of human contrivance is so obvious and natural, and is justified by so many instances of order and design in nature, that it must immediately strike all unprejudiced apprehensions, and procure universal approbation. Whoever attempts to weaken this theory, cannot pretend to succeed by establishing in its place any other, that is precise and determinate: It is sufficient for him, if he starts doubts and difficulties; and by remote and abstract views of things, reach that suspense of judgement, which is here the utmost boundary of his wishes.[81] But besides, that this state of mind is in itself unsatisfactory, it can never be steadily maintained against such striking appearances, as continually engage us into the religious hypothesis. A false, absurd system, human nature, from the force of prejudice, is capable of adhering to, with obstinacy and perseverance: But no system at all, in opposition to a theory, supported by strong and obvious reason, by natural propensity, and by early education, I think it absolutely impossible to maintain or defend.

So little, replied *Philo*, do I esteem this suspense of judgement in the present case to be possible, that I am apt to suspect there enters somewhat of a dispute of words into this controversy, more than is usually imagined. That the works of nature bear a great analogy to the productions of art is evident; and according to all rules of good reasoning, we ought to infer, if we argue at all concerning them, that their causes have a proportional analogy. But as there are also considerable differences, we have reason to suppose a proportional difference in the causes; and in particular ought to attribute a much higher degree of power and energy to the supreme cause than any we have ever observed in mankind. Here then the existence of a DEITY is plainly ascertained by reason; and if we make it a question, whether, on account of these analogies, we can properly call him a *mind* or *intelligence*, notwithstanding the vast difference, which may reasonably be supposed between him and human minds; what is this but a mere verbal controversy? No man can deny the analogies between the effects: To restrain ourselves from inquiring concerning the causes is scarcely possible: From this inquiry, the legitimate conclusion is, that the causes have also an analogy: And if we are not contented with calling the first and supreme cause a GOD or DEITY, but desire to vary the expression; what can we call him but MIND or THOUGHT, to which he is justly supposed to bear a considerable resemblance?

All men of sound reason are disgusted with verbal disputes, which abound so much in philosophical and theological inquiries; and it is found, that the only remedy for this abuse must arise from clear definitions, from the precision of those ideas which enter into any argument, and from the strict and uniform use of those terms which are employed. But there is a species of controversy, which, from the very nature of language and of human ideas, is involved in perpetual ambiguity, and can never, by any precaution or any definitions, be able to reach a reasonable certainty or precision. These are the controversies concerning the degrees of any quality or circumstance. Men may argue to all eternity, whether *Hannibal* be a great, or a very great, or a superlatively great man, what degree of beauty *Cleopatra* possessed, what epithet of praise *Livy* or *Thucydides* is entitled to, without bringing the controversy to any determination. The disputants may here agree in their sense and differ in the terms, or *vice versa*; yet never be able to define their terms, so as to enter into each other's meaning: Because the degrees of these qualities are not, like quantity or number, susceptible of any exact mensuration, which may be the standard in the controversy. That the dispute concerning theism is of this nature, and consequently is merely verbal, or, perhaps, if possible, still more incurably ambiguous, will appear upon the slightest inquiry. I ask the theist, if he does not allow, that there is a great and immeasurable, because incomprehensible, difference between the *human* and the *divine* mind: The more pious he is, the more readily will he assent to the affirmative, and the more will he be disposed to magnify the difference: He will even assert, that the difference is of a nature, which cannot be too much magnified. I next turn to the atheist, who, I assert, is only nominally so, and can never possibly be in earnest; and I ask him, whether from the coherence and apparent sympathy in all the parts of this world, there be not a certain degree of analogy among all the operations of nature, in every situation and in every age; whether the rotting of a turnip, the generation of an animal, and the structure of human thought be not energies that probably bear some remote analogy to each other: It is impossible he can deny it: He will readily acknowledge it. Having obtained this concession, I push him still farther in his retreat; and I ask him, if it be not probable, that the principle which first arranged, and still maintains order in this universe, bears not also some remote inconceivable analogy to the other operations of nature, and among the rest to the economy of human mind and thought. However reluctant, he must give his assent. Where then, cry I to both these antagonists, is the subject of your dispute: The theist allows, that the original intelligence is very different from human reason: The atheist allows that the original principle of order bears some remote analogy to it. Will you quarrel, Gentlemen, about the degrees, and enter into a controversy, which admits not of any precise meaning, nor consequently of any determination. If you should be so obstinate, I should not be surprised to find you insensibly change sides; while the theist on the one hand exaggerates the dissimilarity between the supreme being and frail, imperfect, variable, fleeting, and mortal creatures; and the atheist on the other magnifies the analogy among all the operations of nature, in every period, every situation, and every position. Consider then, where the real point of controversy lies, and if you cannot lay aside your disputes, endeavour, at least, to cure yourselves of your animosity.[82]

And here I must acknowledge, *Cleanthes*, that, as the works of nature have a much greater analogy to the effects of *our* art and contrivance, than to those of *our* benevolence and justice; we have reason to infer that the natural attributes of the deity have a greater resemblance to those of man, than his moral have to human virtues. But what is the consequence? Nothing but this, that the moral qualities of man are more defective in their kind than his natural abilities. For as the supreme being is allowed to be absolutely and entirely perfect, whatever differs most from him departs the farthest from the supreme standard of rectitude and perfection.

It seems evident, that the dispute between the sceptics and dogmatists is entirely verbal, or at least regards only the degrees of doubt and assurance, which we ought to indulge with regard to all reasoning: And such disputes are commonly, at the bottom, verbal and admit not of any precise determination. No philosophical dogmatist denies, that there are difficulties both with regard to the senses and to all science, and that these difficulties are in a regular, logical method, absolutely insolvable. No sceptic denies, that we lie under an absolute necessity, notwithstanding these difficulties, of thinking, and believing, and reasoning with regard to all kinds of subjects, and even of frequently assenting with confidence and security. The only difference, then, between these sects, if they merit that name, is that the sceptic, from habit, caprice, or inclination, insists most on the difficulties; the dogmatist, for like reasons, on the necessity.[83]

These, *Cleanthes*, are my unfeigned sentiments on this subject; and these sentiments, you know, I have ever cherished and maintained. But in proportion to my veneration for true religion, is my abhorrence of vulgar superstitions; and I indulge a peculiar pleasure, I confess, in pushing such principles, sometimes into absurdity, sometimes into impiety. And you are sensible, that all bigots, notwithstanding their great aversion to the latter above the former, are commonly equally guilty of both.

My inclination, replied *Cleanthes*, lies, I own, a contrary way. Religion, however corrupted, is still better than no religion at all. The doctrine of a future state is so strong and necessary a security to morals, that we never ought to abandon or neglect it. For if finite and temporary rewards and punishments have so great an effect, as we daily find: How much greater must be expected from such as are infinite and eternal?

How happens it then, said *Philo*, if vulgar superstition be so salutary to society, that all history abounds so much with accounts of its pernicious consequences on public affairs? Factions, civil wars, persecutions, subversions of government, oppression, slavery; these are the dismal consequences which always attend its prevalence over the minds of men. If the religious spirit be ever mentioned in any historical narration, we are sure to meet afterwards with a detail of the miseries, which attend it. And no period of time can be happier and more prosperous, than those in which it is never regarded or heard of.

The reason of this observation, replied *Cleanthes*, is obvious. The proper office of religion is to regulate the hearts of men, humanize their conduct, infuse the spirit of temperance, order, and obedience; and as its operation is silent, and only enforces the motives of morality and justice, it is in danger of being overlooked, and confounded with these other motives. When it distinguishes itself, and acts as a separate principle over men, it has departed from its proper sphere, and has become only a cover to faction and ambition.

And so will all religion, said *Philo*, except the philosophical and rational kind. Your reasonings are more easily eluded than my facts. The inference is not just, because finite and temporary rewards and punishments have so great influence, that therefore such as are infinite and eternal must have so much greater. Consider, I beseech you, the attachment which we have to present things, and the little concern which we discover for objects so remote and uncertain.[84] When divines are declaiming against the common behaviour and conduct of the world, they always represent this principle the strongest imaginable (which indeed it is), and describe almost all human kind as lying under the influence of it, and sunk into the deepest lethargy and unconcern about their religious interests. Yet these same divines, when they refute their speculative antagonists, suppose the motives of religion to be so powerful, that, without them, it were impossible for civil society to subsist; nor are they ashamed of so palpable a contradiction. It is certain, from experience, that the smallest grain of natural honesty and benevolence has more effect on men's conduct, than the most pompous views, suggested by theological theories and systems. A man's natural inclination works incessantly upon him; it is for ever present to the mind; and mingles itself with every view and consideration:[85] Whereas religious motives, where they act at all, operate only by starts and bounds; and it is scarcely possible for them to become altogether habitual to the mind. The force of the greatest gravity, say the philosophers, is infinitely small, in comparison of that of the least impulse; yet it is certain, that the smallest gravity will, in the end, prevail above a great impulse; because no strokes or blows can be repeated with such constancy as attraction and gravitation.

Another advantage of inclination: It engages on its side all the wit and ingenuity of the mind; and when set in opposition to religious principles, seeks every method and art of eluding them: In which it is almost always successful. Who can explain the heart of man, or account for those strange salvos and excuses, with which people satisfy themselves, when they follow their inclinations in opposition to their religious duty? This is well understood in the world; and none but fools ever repose less trust in a man, because they hear, that, from study and philosophy, he has entertained some speculative doubts with regard to theological subjects. And when we have to do with a man, who makes a great profession of religion and devotion; has this any other effect upon several, who pass for prudent, than to put them on their guard, lest they be cheated and deceived by him?

We must further consider, that philosophers, who cultivate reason and reflection, stand less in need of such motives to keep them under the restraint of morals: And that the vulgar, who alone may need them, are utterly incapable of so pure a religion as represents the deity to be pleased with nothing but virtue in human behaviour. The recommendations to the divinity are generally supposed to be either frivolous observances, or rapturous ecstasies, or a bigoted credulity. We need not run back into antiquity, or wander into remote regions, to find instances of this degeneracy. Amongst ourselves, some have been guilty of that atrociousness, unknown to the Egyptian and Greek superstitions, of declaiming, in express terms, against morality, and representing it as a sure forfeiture of the divine favour, if the least trust or reliance be laid upon it.[86]

But even though superstition or enthusiasm should not put itself in direct opposition to morality; the very diverting of the attention, the raising up a new and frivolous species of merit, the preposterous distribution which it makes of praise and blame; must have the most pernicious consequences, and weaken extremely men's attachment to the natural motives of justice and humanity.

Such a principle of action likewise, not being any of the familiar motives of human conduct, acts only by intervals on the temper, and must be roused by continual efforts, in order to render the pious zealot satisfied with his own conduct, and make him fulfil his devotional task. Many religious exercises are entered into with seeming fervour, where the heart, at the time, feels cold and languid: A habit of dissimulation is by degrees contracted: And fraud and falsehood become the predominate principle. Hence the reason of that vulgar observation, that the highest zeal in religion and the deepest hypocrisy, so far from being inconsistent, are often or commonly united in the same individual character.

The bad effects of such habits, even in common life, are easily imagined: But, where the interests of religion are concerned, no morality can be forcible enough to bind the enthusiastic zealot. The sacredness of the cause sanctifies every measure which can be made use of to promote it.

The steady attention alone to so important an interest as that of eternal salvation is apt to extinguish the benevolent affections, and beget a narrow, contracted selfishness. And when such a temper is encouraged, it easily eludes all the general precepts of charity and benevolence.

Thus the motives of vulgar superstition have no great influence on general conduct; nor is their operation favourable to morality in the instances, where they predominate.[87]

Is there any maxim in politics more certain and infallible, than that both the number and the authority of priests should be confined within very narrow limits, and that the civil magistrate ought, for ever, to keep his *fasces* and *axes* from such dangerous hands? But if the spirit of popular religion were so salutary to society, a contrary maxim ought to prevail. The greater number of priests, and their greater authority and riches will always augment the religious spirit. And though the priests have the guidance of this spirit; why may we not expect a superior sanctity of life, and greater benevolence and moderation, from persons who are set apart for religion, who are continually inculcating it upon others, and who must themselves imbibe a greater share of it? Whence comes it then, that, in fact, the utmost a wise magistrate can propose with regard to popular religions, is, as far as possible, to make a saving game of it, and to prevent their pernicious consequences with regard to society? Every expedient which he tries for so humble a purpose is surrounded with inconveniences. If he admits only one religion among his subjects, he must sacrifice, to an uncertain prospect of tranquillity, every consideration of public liberty, science, reason, industry, and even his own independence. If he gives indulgence to several sects, which is the wiser maxim, he must preserve a very philosophical indifference to all of them, and carefully restrain the pretensions of the prevailing sect; otherwise he can expect nothing but endless disputes, quarrels, factions, persecutions, and civil commotions. True religion, I allow, has no such pernicious consequences:

But we must treat of religion, as it has commonly been found in the world; nor have I any thing to do with that speculative tenet of theism,[88] which, as it is a species of philosophy, must partake of the beneficial influence of that principle, and at the same time must lie under a like inconvenience, of being always confined to a very few persons.[89]

Oaths are requisite in all courts of judicature; but it is a question whether their authority arises from any popular religion. It is the solemnity and importance of the occasion, the regard to reputation, and the reflecting on the general interests of society, which are the chief restraints upon mankind. Custom-house oaths and political oaths are but little regarded even by some who pretend to principles of honesty and religion: And a Quaker's asseveration is with us justly put upon the same footing with the oath of any other person. I know that *Polybius** ascribes the infamy of Greek faith to the prevalence of the Epicurean philosophy; but I know also, that Punic faith had as bad a reputation in ancient times, as Irish evidence has in modern; though we cannot account for these vulgar observations by the same reason. Not to mention, that Greek faith was infamous before the rise of the Epicurean philosophy; and *Euripides*,† in a passage which I shall point out to you, has glanced a remarkable stroke of satire against his nation, with regard to this circumstance.

Take care, *Philo*, replied *Cleanthes*, take care: Push not matters too far: Allow not your zeal against false religion to undermine your veneration for the true. Forfeit not this principle, the chief, the only great comfort in life; and our principal support amidst all the attacks of adverse fortune. The most agreeable reflection, which it is possible for human imagination to suggest, is that of genuine theism, which represents us as the workmanship of a being perfectly good, wise, and powerful; who created us for happiness, and who, having implanted in us immeasurable desires of good, will prolong our existence to all eternity, and will transfer us into an infinite variety of scenes, in order to satisfy those desires, and render our felicity complete and durable. Next to

* Lib. 6 Cap. 54[90]
† *Iphigenia in Tauride*[91]

such a being himself (if the comparison be allowed) the happiest lot which we can imagine, is that of being under his guardianship and protection.[92]

These appearances, said *Philo*, are most engaging and alluring; and with regard to the true philosopher, they are more than appearances. But it happens here, as in the former case, that, with regard to the greater part of mankind, the appearances are deceitful, and that the terrors of religion commonly prevail above its comforts.

It is allowed, that men never have recourse to devotion so readily as when dejected with grief or depressed with sickness. Is not this a proof, that the religious spirit is not so nearly allied to joy as to sorrow?

But men, when afflicted, find consolation in religion, replied *Cleanthes*. Sometimes, said *Philo*: But it is natural to imagine, that they will form a notion of those unknown beings, suitable to the present gloom and melancholy of their temper, when they betake themselves to the contemplation of them. Accordingly, we find the tremendous images to predominate in all religions; and we ourselves, after having employed the most exalted expression in our descriptions of the deity, fall into the flattest contradiction, in affirming that the damned are infinitely superior in number to the elect.[93]

I shall venture to affirm, that there never was a popular religion, which represented the state of departed souls in such a light, as would render it eligible for human kind, that there should be such a state. These fine models of religion are the mere product of philosophy. For as death lies between the eye and the prospect of futurity, that event is so shocking to nature, that it must throw a gloom on all the regions, which lie beyond it; and suggest to the generality of mankind the idea of *Cerberus* and Furies; devils, and torrents of fire and brimstone.

It is true; both fear and hope enter into religion; because both these passions, at different times, agitate the human mind, and each of them forms a species of divinity, suitable to itself. But when a man is in a cheerful disposition, he is fit for business, or company, or entertainment of any kind; and he naturally applies himself to these, and thinks not of religion. When melancholy, and dejected, he has nothing to do but brood upon the terrors of the invisible world, and to plunge himself still deeper in affliction. It may, indeed, happen, that after he has, in this manner engraved the religious opinions deep into his thought and imagination, there may arrive a change of health or circumstances, which may restore his good humour, and raising cheerful prospects of futurity, make him run into the other extreme of joy and triumph. But still it must be acknowledged, that, as terror is the primary principle of all religion, it is the passion, which always predominates in it, and admits but of short intervals of pleasure.[94]

Not to mention, that these fits of excessive, enthusiastic joy, by exhausting the spirits, always prepare the way for equal fits of superstitious terror and dejection; nor is there any state of mind so happy as the calm and equable. But this state it is impossible to support, where a man thinks, that he lies in such profound darkness and uncertainty, between an eternity of happiness and an eternity of misery. No wonder, that such an opinion disjoints the ordinary frame of the mind, and throws it into the utmost confusion. And though that opinion is seldom so steady in its operation as to influence all the actions; yet it is apt to make a considerable breach in the temper, and to produce that gloom and melancholy, so remarkable in all devout people.

It is contrary to common sense to entertain apprehensions or terrors, upon account of any opinion whatsoever, or to imagine that we run any risk hereafter, by the freest use of our reason.[95] Such a sentiment implies both an *absurdity* and an *inconsistency*. It is an absurdity to believe the deity has human passions, and one of the lowest of human passions, a restless appetite for applause. It is an inconsistency to believe, that, since the deity has this human passion, he has not others also; and in particular, a disregard to the opinions of creatures so much inferior.

To know God, says Seneca, *is to worship him*.[96] All other worship is indeed absurd, superstitious, and even impious. It degrades him to the low condition of mankind, who are delighted with entreaty, solicitation, presents, and flattery. Yet is this impiety the smallest of which superstition is guilty. Commonly, it depresses the deity far below the condition of mankind, and represents him as a capricious demon, who exercises his power without reason and without humanity. And were that divine being disposed to be offended at the vices and follies of silly mortals, who are his own workmanship; ill would it surely fare with the votaries of most popular superstitions. Nor would any of human race merit his *favour*, but a very few, the philosophical theists, who entertain, or rather indeed endeavour to entertain, suitable notions of his divine perfections: As the only persons, entitled to his *compassion* and *indulgence*, would be the philosophical sceptics, a sect almost equally rare, who, from a natural diffidence of their own capacity, suspend, or endeavour to suspend all judgement with regard to such sublime and such extraordinary subjects.

If the whole of natural theology, as some people seem to maintain, resolves itself into one simple, though somewhat ambiguous, at least undefined, proposition, *that the cause or causes of order in the universe probably bear some remote analogy to human intelligence*: If this proposition be not capable of extension, variation, or more particular explication: If it affords no inference that affects human life, or can be the source of any action or forbearance: And if the analogy, imperfect as it is, can be carried no farther than to human intelligence; and cannot be transferred, with any appearance of probability, to the other qualities of the mind: If this really be the case, what can the most inquisitive, contemplative, and religious man do more than give a plain, philosophical assent to the proposition, as often as it occurs; and believe, that the arguments, on which it is established, exceed the objections, which lie against it? Some astonishment indeed will naturally arise from the greatness of the object: Some melancholy from its obscurity: Some contempt of human reason, that it can give no solution more satisfactory with regard to so extraordinary and magnificent a question. But believe me, *Cleanthes*, the most natural sentiment, which a well disposed mind will feel on this occasion, is a longing desire and expectation, that heaven would be pleased to dissipate, at least alleviate this profound ignorance, by affording some more particular revelation to mankind, and making discoveries of the nature, attributes, and operations of the divine object of our faith. A person, seasoned with a just sense of the imperfections of natural reason, will fly to revealed truth with the greater avidity: While the haughty dogmatist, persuaded, that he can erect a complete system of theology by the mere help of philosophy,[97] disdains any farther aid, and rejects this adventitious instructor. To be a philosophical sceptic is, in a man of letters, the first and most essential step towards being a sound, believing *Christian*;[98] a proposition, which I would willingly recommend to the attention of *Pamphilus*: and I hope *Cleanthes* will forgive me for interposing so far in the education and instruction of his pupil.

Cleanthes and *Philo* pursued not this conversation much farther; and as nothing ever made greater impression on me, than all the reasonings of that day; so, I confess, that, upon a serious review of the whole, I cannot but think, that *Philo's* principles are more probable than *Demea's*; but that those of *Cleanthes* approach still nearer to the truth.[99]

NOTES

1. (p. 40) The reference is to 'De Stoicorum Repugnantiis' ('On Stoic Self-contradictions') in Plutarch, *Moralia*: 'Chrysippus thinks that young men should hear lectures on logic first, on ethics next, and after that on physics and should get theology last as the termination for these studies.' Trans. H. Cherniss, Loeb, London, 1976, p. 429.

2. (p. 43) Compare T.316: 'Most fortunately it happens, that since reason is incapable of dispelling these clouds, nature herself suffices to that purpose, and cures me of this philosophical melancholy and delirium, either by relaxing this bent of mind, or by some avocation, and lively impression of my senses, which obliterate all these chimeras.'

3. (p. 43) See Introduction, p. 24.

4. (p. 43) Stoicism was a school of philosophy founded by Zeno of Citium (344–262 BC), whose successor as head of the school was Cleanthes (died c.232 BC). A subsequent leading Stoic, Diodatus, taught Cicero. Rivalry between Stoics and Sceptics was a feature of Hellenistic philosophy. Stoics believed that knowledge, of a kind needed for us to lead a rational and happy life, is achievable, while Sceptics doubted that a criterion of knowledge can be given.

5. (p. 43) See Hume, 'The Stoic', in *Essays: Moral, Political and Literary*, especially pp. 153–4: 'GLORY is the portion of virtue, the sweet reward of honourable toils, the triumphant crown, which covers the thoughtful head of the disinterested patriot, or the dusty brow of the victorious warrior. Elevated by so sublime a prize, the man of virtue looks down with contempt on all the allurements of pleasure, and all the menaces of danger.'

6. (p. 44) John Milton, *Paradise Lost*, ii, 565–9.

7. (p. 44) Compare T.318: 'I cannot forbear having a curiosity to be acquainted with the principles of moral good and evil, the nature and foundation of government, and the cause of those several passions and inclinations, which actuate and govern me . . . I feel an ambition to arise in me of contributing to the instruction of mankind, and of acquiring a name by my inventions and discoveries. These sentiments spring up naturally in my present disposition; and shou'd I endeavour to banish them, by attaching myself to any other business or diversion, I *feel* I shou'd be a loser in point of pleasure; and this is the origin of my philosophy.'

8. (*p. 44*) Compare: 'Those who have a propensity to philosophy, will still continue their researches; because they reflect, that, besides the immediate pleasure, attending such an occupation, philosophical decisions are nothing but the reflections of common life, methodized and corrected.' E.162. References of the form 'E.n' are to page n. of Hume, *An Enquiry Concerning Human Understanding*, in the edition listed in the Select Bibliography.

9. (*p. 46*) Sir Isaac Newton (1642–1727). His *Opticks: or, a treatise of the refractions, inflections and colours of light* was published in 1704.

10. (*p. 46*) Nicholas Copernicus (1473–1543). His *De revolutionibus orbium coelestium* (*On the revolutions of the heavenly spheres*) was published in 1543. It proposed the heliocentric theory of the universe, replacing the geocentric theory of Ptolemy. The *Dialogo sopra i due massimi sistemi del mondo* (*Dialogue concerning the two chief world systems*) by Galileo Galilei (1564–1642) was published in 1632. This compared the Ptolemaic and Copernican theories.

11. (*p. 47*) *La Logique, ou l'art de penser* (*The Art of Thinking*; also known as the *Port-Royal Logic*) by Antoine Arnauld (1612–94) and Pierre Nicol (1625–95) was published in 1662.

12. (*p. 48*) Pierre-Daniel Huet (1630–1721), Bishop of Avranches. Author of a sceptical work, *Traité philosophique de la faiblesse de l'esprit humain* (*A Philosophical Treatise on the Weakness of Human Understanding*) published in 1723.

13. (*p. 49*) John Locke (1632–1704) published, anonymously, *The Reasonableness of Christianity* in 1695.

14. (*p. 49*) Pierre Bayle (1674–1706) was a leading sceptic. Hume refers to articles in Bayle's *Dictionnaire historique et critique* (*Historical and Critical Dictionary*). This massive, rambling work was first published in 1697, and is a treasure-house of sceptical arguments. For a recent assessment of Bayle, see Elisabeth Labrousse, *Bayle*, Oxford, 1983.

15. (*p. 49*) The essay 'Of Atheism' in *Essays*, published in 1597, by Francis Bacon (1561–1626). Compare also: 'A little philosophy, says lord BACON, *makes men atheists: A great deal reconciles them to religion*. For men, being taught, by superstitious prejudices, to lay stress on a wrong place; when that fails them, and they discover, by a little reflection, that the course of nature is regular and uniform, their whole faith totters, and falls to ruin. But being taught, by more reflection, that this very regularity and uniformity is the strongest proof of design and of a supreme intelligence, they return to that belief, which they had deserted; and they are now able to establish it on a firmer and more durable foundation' (NHR.42). References of the form 'NHR.n' are to page n. of *The Natural History of Religion*, in the edition listed in the Select Bibliography.

16. (*p. 49*) Psalm XIV:1.

17. (*p. 50*) Platonists were followers of Plato, and Peripatetics, of Aristotle.

18. (*p. 51*) 1 Corinthians II:9.

19. (*p. 52*) Nicolas Malebranche (1638–1715). His *De la recherche de la vérité* (*The Search after Truth*) was originally published in 1674–5, and

was in a sixth edition by 1712. For the influence of Malebranche on Hume, among others, see C. J. McCraken, *Malebranche and British Philosophy*, Oxford, 1983.

20. (*p. 52*)   Exodus III:14.

21. (*p. 53*)   Argument *a posteriori*: an argument, often inductive, from factual premisses established by observation and experience.

22. (*p. 54*)   Proof *a priori*: a deductive derivation of a conclusion from premisses which are logically or conceptually true. For the variety of uses of *a priori* and *a posteriori* in eighteenth-century authors, see J. P. Ferguson, *The Philosophy of Dr Samuel Clarke and its Critics*, New York, 1974, Chapter 2.

23. (*p. 55*)   The *final* cause of a process is the end result achieved, which is thought of as the purpose or aim of the process. The notion of final causes is Aristotelian in origin. For Hume's rejection of the Aristotelian classification of causes, see T.221.

24. (*p. 56*)   Compare E.25–32.

25. (*p. 57*)   'There is no phaenomenon in nature, but what is compounded and modify'd by so many different circumstances, that in order to arrive at the decisive point, we must carefully separate whatever is superfluous, and enquire by new experiments, if every particular circumstance of the first experiment was essential to it. These new experiments are liable to a discussion of the same kind; so that the utmost constancy is requir'd to make us persevere in our enquiry, and the utmost sagacity to choose the right way among so many that present themselves.' T.225.

26. (*p. 59*)   *animalcule*: literally, a tiny animal. It used to be thought that sperm contains a tiny but complete offspring.

27. (*p. 60*)   Simonides (550–470 BC), lyric poet. Hiero, tyrant of Syracuse. The story is in Cicero, *De Natura Deorum*, I, xxii.

28. (*p. 61*)   Galileo's *Dialogue* (see Note 10, above) has three characters, one supporting the Copernican theory, a second defending the Aristotelian and Ptolemaic conception, and a third, an intelligent layman, who gives his assent to the arguments of the supporter of Copernicus. See the modern translation by S. Drake, *Dialogue Concerning the Two Chief World Systems*, Berkeley, 1953.

29. (*p. 65*)   'In all the incidents of life we ought still to preserve our scepticism. If we believe, that fire warms, or water refreshes, 'tis only because it costs us too much pains to think otherwise … Where reason is lively, and mixes itself with some propensity, it ought to be assented to. Where it does not, it never can have any title to operate upon us.' T.317.

30. (*p. 66*)   For the origin of this passage in the writings of the Newtonian, Colin Maclaurin (1698–1746), see the Introduction, Note 21.

31. (*p. 66*)   In a letter of 1751, Hume asked Gilbert Elliot of Minto to help him strengthen Cleanthes' position; and he acknowledged his own tendency towards the view of Philo. He continued: 'And 'tis not long ago that I burn'd an old Manuscript Book, wrote before I was twenty; which contain'd, Page after Page, the gradual progress of

my Thoughts on that head. It begun with an anxious Search after Arguments, to confirm the common Opinion: Doubts stole in, dissipated, return'd, were again dissipated, return'd again; and it was a perpetual Struggle of a restless Imagination against Inclination, perhaps against Reason.' J. Y. T. Greig (ed.), *The Letters of David Hume*, Oxford, 1932, Vol. 1, p. 154.

32. (p. 67) Again Hurlbutt (see Note 30) has found the origin of this passage in Maclaurin. Plotinus (AD 205–270) was a Roman neo-Platonist whose writings were collected by Porphyry, in the *Enneads*.

33. (p. 70) Hume describes the soul, or self, as '. . . nothing but a bundle or collection of different perceptions, which succeed each other with an inconceivable rapidity, and are in a perpetual flux and movement.' T.300.

34. (p. 71) In Cicero's *De Natura Deorum* the Epicurean, Velleius, puts such an argument: 'For the belief in the gods has not been established by authority, custom or law, but rests on the unanimous and abiding consensus of mankind; their existence is therefore a necessary inference, since we possess an instinctive or rather innate concept of them; but a belief which all men by nature share must necessarily be true; therefore it must be admitted that the gods exist.' Trans. H. Rackham, Loeb, London, 1933, p. 45.

For the assertion that idolaters are atheists, see NHR.33: 'To any one, who considers justly of the matter, it will appear, that the gods of all polytheists are not better than the elves or fairies of our ancestors, and merit as little any pious worship or veneration. These pretended religionists are really a kind of superstitious atheists, and acknowledge no being, that corresponds to our idea of a deity.'

35. (p. 72) 'Had the poor Indian philosopher (who imagined that the earth also wanted something to bear it up) but thought of this word *substance*, he needed not to have been at the trouble to find an elephant to support it, and a tortoise to support his elephant: the word *substance* would have done it effectually.' John Locke, *An Essay Concerning Human Understanding*, ed. P. H. Nidditch, Oxford, 1975, 2, 13, 19.

36. (p. 74) In Cicero, *De Natura Deorum*, the Stoic, Balbus, says: 'For when we gaze upward to the sky and contemplate the heavenly bodies, what can be so obvious and so manifest as that there must exist some power possessing transcendent intelligence by whom these things are ruled? Were it not so, how comes it that the words of Ennius carry conviction to all readers –

Behold this dazzling vault of heaven, which
all mankind as Jove invoke

ay, and not only as Jove but as the sovereign of the world, ruling all things with his nod, and as Ennius likewise says –

father of gods and men,

a deity omnipresent and omnipotent? If a man doubts this, I really cannot see why he should not also be capable of doubting the existence of the sun; how is the latter fact more evident than the former?' Op. cit., pp. 125–7.

37. (p. 75) Titus Lucretius Carus (c.99–55 BC) wrote *De Rerum Natura* (*On the Nature of Things*), a poem expounding Epicureanism. Epicurus (341–270 BC), Greek philosopher and scientist, was taught as a boy by the Platonist, Pamphilus, and studied at the Academy. He settled in Athens, and taught in the Gardens. Our knowledge of Epicureanism is largely dependent on Lucretius. The passage quoted means: 'Who is strong enough to rule the sum of the immeasurable, who to hold in hand and control the mighty bridle of the unfathomable? who to turn about all the heavens at one time and warm the fruitful worlds with ethereal fires, or to be present in all places and at all times'. Trans. W. H. D. Rouse, revised M. Ferguson Smith, Loeb, London, 1975, p. 181.

38. (p. 75) 'What power of mental vision enabled your master Plato to descry the vast and elaborate architectural process which, as he makes out, the deity adopted in building the structure of the universe? What method of engineering was employed? What tools and levers and derricks? What agents carried out so vast an undertaking? And how were air, fire, water and earth enabled to obey and execute the will of the architect?' Cicero, op. cit., trans. H. Rackham, p. 23.

Hume often used 'Tully' as a name of Marcus Tullius Cicero.

39. (p. 76) Compare: 'I shall only observe this one thing, that the greater the improvements and discoveries are, which are daily made in astronomy and natural philosophy; the more clearly is this question [whether the supreme cause of all things is a being indued with liberty and choice] continually determined, to the shame and confusion of atheists.' Samuel Clarke, *A Demonstration of the Being and Attributes of God*, p. 142.

40. (p. 76) Compare the attack on anthropomorphism by the Sceptic, Cotta, in *De Natura Deorum*: 'You don't perceive what a number of things you are let in for, if we consent to admit that men and gods have the same form.' Cicero, op. cit., p. 93.

41. (p. 77) Compare: ''Tis evident therefore, that the self-existent being must be infinite in the *strictest* and most *complete* sense. But now as to the particular *manner* of his being infinite . . . it is as impossible for our finite understandings, to comprehend or explain; as it is for us to form an adequate idea of infinity.' Samuel Clarke, op. cit., p. 91.

42. (p. 78) John Milton, *Paradise Lost*, viii, 150–1.

43. (p. 78) See the Epicurean argument: '. . . since it is agreed that the gods are supremely happy, and no one can be happy without virtue, and virtue cannot exist without reason, and reason is only found in the human shape, it follows that the gods possess the form of man.' Cicero, op. cit., p. 49.

44. (p. 81) For example: 'As for Pythagoras, who believed that the entire substance of the universe is penetrated and pervaded by a soul . . . Next, Xenophanes endowed the universe with mind, and held that, as being infinite, it was god.' Cicero, op. cit., p. 31.

45. (p. 83) L. Licinius Lucullus (c. 110–57 BC), Roman general, famous as the

conqueror of Mithradates. He obtained great wealth from his campaigns in Asia, and was renowned for his lavish life style. See the introductory sections of Cicero, *Academica*, II.

46. (*p. 84*) '. . . 'tis commonly allow'd by philosophers, that what the vulgar call chance is nothing but a secret and conceal'd cause.' T.181.

47. (*p. 85*) Hesiod (*c.* 700 BC), one of the oldest known Greek poets. The *Theogony*, one of his two major poems to have survived, gives an account of the gods of Greece and their genealogy. See also NHR. 28, n.1.

48. (*p. 88*) Compare: 'It is confessed, that the utmost effort of human reason is to reduce the principles, productive of natural phenomena, to a greater simplicity, and to resolve the many particular effects into a few general causes, by means of reasonings from analogy, experience, and observation. But as to the causes of these general causes, we should in vain attempt their discovery . . .' E.30.

49. (*p. 90*) Plato, *Timaeus*, 29d–31g.

50. (*p. 91*) Compare: 'While a warm imagination is allow'd to enter into philosophy, and hypotheses embrac'd merely for being specious and agreeable, we can never have any steady principles, nor any sentiments, which will suit with common practice and experience.' T.319.

   Also: 'But that all his arguments, though otherwise intended, are, in reality, merely sceptical, appears from this, *that they admit of no answer and produce no conviction.* Their only effect is to cause that momentary amazement and irresolution and confusion, which is the result of scepticism.' E.155, n.1.

51. (*p. 92*) 'Thus the wise man will make use of whatever apparently probable presentation he encounters, if nothing presents itself that is contrary to that probability, and his whole plan of life will be charted out in this manner.' Cicero, op. cit., p. 595.

52. (*p. 92*) 'A correct *judgment* . . . avoiding all distant and high enquiries, confines itself to common life, and to such subjects as fall under daily practice and experience.' E.162.

53. (*p. 92*) 'While we cannot give a satisfactory reason, why we believe, after a thousand experiments, that a stone will fall, or fire burn; can we ever satisfy ourselves concerning any determination, which we may form, with regard to the origin of worlds, and the situation of nature, from, and to eternity.' *Idem.*

54. (*p. 92*) In the system of Epicurus, the atoms (*primordia*) '. . . being many and shifted in many ways, they are harried and set in motion with blows throughout the universe from infinity, thus by trying every kind of motion and combination, at length they fall into such arrangements as this sum of things consists of . . .' Lucretius, op. cit., p. 85.

55. (*p. 92*) 'At this point must I not marvel that there should be anyone who can persuade himself . . . that the fortuitous collision of . . . particles produces this elaborate and beautiful world?' Cicero, op. cit., p. 213.

   See also, Samuel Clarke, op. cit., p. 119.

56. (p. 96) Compare Cicero, op. cit., II, lxii–lxiv.
57. (p. 97) 'Doubt, uncertainty, suspense of judgment appear the only result of our most accurate scrutiny, concerning this subject.' NHR. 76.
58. (p. 98) '. . . therefore I shall not at this time use any variety of arguments, but endeavour by one clear and plain series of propositions necessarily connected and following one from another, to demonstrate the certainty of the being of God, and to deduce in order the necessary attributes of his nature . . .' Samuel Clarke, op. cit., p. 16.
59. (p. 99) 'Whatever exists, has a cause of its existence, either in the necessity of its own nature; and then it must have been eternal: or in the will of some other being; and then that other being must, at least in the order of nature and causality have existed before it . . . Either there has always existed one unchangeable and independent being, from which all other beings that are or ever were in the universe, have received their original; or else there has been an infinite succession of changeable and dependent beings . . . which latter supposition is so very absurd . . .' idem., pp. 18–19, 23–4.
60. (p. 99) See above, Introduction, p. 18.
61. (p. 100) 'Now that the material world does not exist thus necessarily, is evident . . . For whether we consider the form of the world, with the disposition and motion of its parts; or whether we consider the matter of it, as such, without respect to its present form; every thing in it, both the whole and every one of its parts, their situation and motion, the form and also the matter, are the most arbitrary and dependent things . . . If he [the atheist] says that the particular form is necessary; he must affirm it to be a contradiction to suppose that any part of the world can be in any respect otherwise than it now is . . .' Samuel Clarke, op. cit., pp. 43–5.
62. (p. 101) See T.121–6.
63. (p. 104) Perhaps a reference to Edward Young (1683–1765).
64. (p. 104) Gottfried Wilhelm Leibniz (1641–1716) had maintained that in creating the world, God creates the best of all possible worlds. (See his Theodicy, trans. E. M. Huggard, ed. A. Farrer, London, 1951.)

Dr King is William King (1650–1729), Archbishop of Dublin, and author of De Origine Mali (1702). A translation of this by Edmund Law, An Essay on the Origin of Evil, was published in London in 1732.

Anders Jeffner (Butler and Hume on Religion, Stockholm, 1966, p. 151) points out that neither Leibniz nor King deny the existence of human misery; and that there are similarities between King's description of evil and that given below by Demea, beginning 'The whole earth . . . is cursed and polluted'.
65. (p. 105) Compare, Hume, 'Of Superstition and Enthusiasm', loc. cit.
66. (p. 106) John Milton, Paradise Lost, xi, 484–93, omitting line 488.
67. (p. 106) 'Monuments to human misery and wickedness are found everywhere – prisons, hospitals, gallows, and beggars. Here you see the ruins of a flourishing city; in other places you cannot even find the ruins . . . Properly speaking, history is nothing but the crimes and misfortunes of the human race.' Bayle, op. cit., 'Manicheans'.

68. (*p. 108*) Charles V (1500–1558), King of Spain and Holy Roman Emperor, resigned his thrones in 1556 and 1558. Hume is quoting from the article on Charles V in Bayle, op. cit.

69. (*p. 108*) Probably a reference to Cicero, *De Senectute* (*On Old Age*), xxiii, 83–4, where Cato says: 'Nay, if some god should give me leave to return to infancy from my old age, to weep once more in my cradle, I should vehemently protest; for truly, after I have run my race I have no wish to be recalled, as it were, from the goal to the starting-place. For what advantage has life – or, rather, what trouble does it not have?' Trans. W. A. Falconer, Loeb, London, 1923.

70. (*p. 108*) John Dryden, *Aureng-Zebe*, iv, i, 41–2. Hume has 'hope' in place of 'think'.

71. (*p. 109*) Compare Bayle, op. cit., 'Paulicians'. This whole speech by Philo shows the influence of Bayle's discussion of the problem of evil. Like Bayle, Philo opposes anthropomorphic theodicies, and declares that reason can provide no solution.

72. (*p. 109*) 'For example, if you say that God has permitted sin in order to manifest his wisdom, which shines forth more in the midst of the disorders that man's wickedness produces every day than it would in a state of innocence, you will be answered that this is to compare God either to a father who allows his children to break their legs so that he can show everyone his great skill in mending their broken bones, or to a king who allows seditions and disorders to develop through his kingdom so that he can gain glory by overcoming them. The conduct of this father and this monarch is so contrary to the clear and distinct ideas by which we judge goodness and wisdom and in general all the duties of a father and a king, that our reason cannot conceive how God could act in this way. But, you will say, the ways of God are not our ways. Stop at this point, it is a text of scripture [Isaiah 55:8], and do not reason any further.' Bayle, op. cit., 'Paulicians'.

73. (*p. 112*) 'One does not have to be a metaphysician to know this . . . All of this warns us that we should not dispute . . . until we have established the doctrine of the *elevation of faith and the abasement of reason.*' *Idem.*

74. (*p. 113*) For a discussion of the problems, outlined here by Cleanthes, for a natural theology which argues from analogy, and some historical background to Hume's treatment, see Anders Jeffner, op. cit., pp. 200ff.

75. (*p. 117*) In Hume's manuscript there is here a deleted note: '*Caesar*, speaking of the woods in Germany, mentions some animals as subsisting there, which are now utterly extinct. These, and some few more instances, may be exceptions to the proposition here delivered. *Strabo* quotes from *Polybius* an account of an animal about the Tyrol, which is not now to be found. If *Polybius* was not deceived, which is possible, the animal must have been then very rare, since *Strabo* cites but one authority, and speaks doubtfully.'

Hume's sources can be found in Caesar, *De Bello Gallico* (*The*

Gallic War), vi, 26–8, and *The Geography of Strabo*, trans. H. L. Jones, Loeb, London, 1923, Vol. II, p. 289.

76. (*p. 121*) The Manicheans were a sect who taught that the universe is governed by two independent principles, one the source of good, the other the source of evil. This heresy was opposed by St Augustine, who had earlier been an adherent. Bayle's account of the Manicheans is an important source for Hume in this part. Philo's view that the evil in the world presents an insuperable obstacle for natural theology based on *a posteriori* reasoning is reminiscent of Bayle's statement about the Manicheans: 'They would soon have been defeated by *a priori* arguments; their strength lay in *a posteriori* arguments. With these they could have fought a long time, and it would have been difficult to defeat them.'

77. (*p. 122*) There is here again an echo of Bayle. His unflinching refusal to accept any theodicy which tries to explain away the fact that God creates a universe containing sin and suffering opened him to the accusation, also made against Calvin, that he portrayed God as the author of sin. See Labrousse, op. cit., pp. 61–8. It is this implication that horrifies Demea.

78. (*p. 126*) With Philo's statement that his intentions will not be mistaken by anyone of common sense, compare Bayle, op. cit., 'Clarifications', the general and preliminary observation. For the similarity between Bayle and Philo on the claim that 'the divine being ... discovers himself to reason, in the inexplicable contrivance and artifice of nature', see Labrousse, op. cit., pp. 54–6.

See also: 'The whole frame of nature bespeaks an intelligent author; and no rational enquirer can, after serious reflection, suspend his belief a moment with regard to the primary principles of genuine theism and religion.' NHR.21.

79. (*p. 126*) Claudius Galen, (AD 131–200), Greek physician. He studied in Smyrna and Alexandria, and practised in Rome, becoming personal physician of the emperor, Marcus Aurelius. He wrote extensively on anatomy and the theory of science and medicine. The work to which Hume refers is 'On the formation of the foetus'.

80. (*p. 127*) 'If *Galen* so many ages ago, could find in the construction and constitution of the parts of the human body, such undeniable marks of contrivance and design; as forced him *then* to acknowledge and admire the wisdom of its author; what would he have said, if he had known the *late* discoveries in anatomy and physic, the circulation of the blood, the exact structure of the heart and brain, the uses of numberless glands and valves for the secretion and motion of the juices in the body, besides several veins and other vessels and receptacles not at all known, or imagined so much as to have any existence, *in his days*.' Samuel Clarke, op. cit., pp. 226–7.

81. (*p. 127*) Compare Part I, above: '... it is that very suspense or balance, which is the triumph of scepticism.'

82. (*p. 130*) 'The greater part of mankind are naturally apt to be affirmative and dogmatical in their opinions ... But could such dogmatical reasoners become sensible of the strange infirmities of human

understanding, even in its most perfect state, and when most accurate and cautious in its determinations; such a reflection would naturally inspire them with more modesty and reserve, and diminish their fond opinion of themselves, and their prejudice against antagonists.' E.161.

83. (p. 130) 'The conduct of a man, who studies philosophy in this careless manner, is more truly sceptical than that of one, who feeling in himself an inclination to it, is yet so over-whelm'd with doubts and scruples, as totally to reject it. A true sceptic will be diffident of his philosophical doubts, as well as of his philosophical conviction; and will never refuse any innocent satisfaction, which offers itself, upon account of either of them.' T.320.

It seems evident . . . on the necessity: This paragraph originally appeared in Hume's manuscript as a note. Hume later deleted it, and rewrote it at the end of the manuscript. In the printed edition of 1779, it appears as a note; and later editors have followed that precedent. But J. V. Price has pointed out that the manuscript instructions to do this do not seem to be in Hume's handwriting; and I agree with his reasons for incorporating it into the text. See A. W. Colver and J. V. Price (eds.), 1976, p. 250, n. 5.

84. (p. 132) 'The world is full of people who prefer to commit a sin rather than displease a prince who can make or break their fortunes. People every day sign formularies of faith against their conscience in order to safeguard their wealth or to avoid jail, exile, death, or the like.' Bayle, op. cit., 'First Clarification'.

85. (p. 132) 'The fabric and constitution of our mind no more depends on our choice, than that of our body . . . As a stream necessarily follows the several inclinations of the ground, on which it runs; so are the ignorant and thoughtless part of mankind actuated by their natural propensities.' Hume, 'The Sceptic', in *Essays: Moral, Political and Literary*.

86. (p. 133) 'In a little time, the inspired person comes to regard himself as a distinguished favourite of the Divinity; and when this frenzy once takes place, which is the summit of enthusiasm, every whimsy is consecrated: Human reason, and even morality are rejected as fallacious guides . . .' 'Of Superstition and Enthusiasm', loc. cit.

87. (p. 134) Compare NHR. *passim*, but especially pp. 70–3.

88. (p. 135) 'The religious philosophers . . . paint, in the most magnificent colours, the order, beauty, and wise arrangement of the universe, and then ask, if such a glorious display of intelligence could proceed from the fortuitous concourse of atoms, or if chance could produce what the greatest genius can never sufficiently admire. I shall not examine the justness of this argument. I shall allow it to be as solid as my antagonists and accusers can desire. It is sufficient, if I can prove, from this very reasoning, that the question is entirely speculative.' E.135.

89. (p. 135) 'What a noble privilege is it of human reason to attain the knowledge of the supreme Being; and, from the visible works of nature, be enabled to infer so sublime a principle as its supreme Creator? But

turn the reverse of the medal. Survey most nations and most ages. Examine the religious principles, which have, in fact, prevailed in the world. You will scarcely be persuaded, that they are any thing but sick men's dreams.' NHR.75.

90. (*p. 135*) The reference that Hume gives to the *Histories* of Polybius does not seem to be accurate. He may have had in mind Book 6, Chapter 56, sections 6–12, where Polybius approves the Roman use of religion for maintaining the cohesion of the state, and criticizes 'the moderns' (he does not mention Epicureans as such) who, in undermining religious beliefs, have, among the Greeks, produced people who cannot be trusted.

91. (*p. 135*) Euripides, *Iphigenia in Tauris*, probably first presented in 414 BC. Hume possibly had in mind the scene in which Iphigenia fools Thoas, using her sanctity as a priestess to cover her lies, and in the course of her deception remarks that 'Greeks are never to be trusted'.

92. (*p. 136*) 'Whether therefore the being and attributes of God can be *demonstrated* or not; it must at least be confessed by all rational and wise men, to be a thing very *desirable*, and which they would heartily *wish* to be true, that there were a God, intelligent and wise, a just and good being, to govern the world.' Samuel Clarke, op. cit., p. 10.

93. (*p. 136*) 'Without having read the fine treatise of Seneca on benefits, everyone knows by the natural light that it is essential to a benefactor not to bestow gifts that he knows will be abused in such a manner that they will only serve to bring about the ruin of the person to whom they are given.' Bayle, op. cit., 'Paulicians'.

94. (*p. 137*) 'Any of the human affections may lead us into the notion of invisible, intelligent power; hope as well as fear, gratitude as well as affliction: But if we examine our own hearts, or observe what passes around us, we shall find, that men are much oftener thrown on their knees by the melancholy than by the agreeable passions.' NHR.31.

95. (*p. 137*) Compare Philo, at the beginning of this Part: '. . . no one, I am confident, in whose eyes I appear a man of common sense will ever mistake my intentions.'

96. (*p. 137*) Seneca, *Epistulae Morales*, xcv, 50: '*Primus est deorum cultus deos credere*'; that is, 'The first way to worship the gods is to believe in the gods', translation by R. M. Gummere, *The Epistles of Seneca*, Loeb, London, 1925, Vol. III, p. 89.

97. (*p. 139*) 'I proceed now to the main thing I at first proposed to my self; namely, to endeavour to show . . . that the being and attributes of God, are not only possible or barely probable in themselves, but also strictly demonstrable to any unprejudiced mind from the most uncontestable principles of reason.' Samuel Clarke, op. cit., p. 14.

98. (*p. 139*) 'This is a great step toward the Christian religion; for it requires that we look to God for knowledge of what we ought to believe and what we ought to do, and that we enslave our understanding to the obeisance of faith. If a man is convinced that nothing good is to be expected from his philosophical enquiries, he will be more disposed to pray to God to persuade him of the truths that ought to be

believed than if he flatters himself that he might succeed by reasoning and disputing. A man is therefore happily disposed toward faith when he knows how defective reason is.' Bayle, op. cit., 'Pyrrho'.

99. (p. 139) 'Here the conversation ended, and we parted, Velleius thinking Cotta's discourse to be truer, while I felt that that of Balbus approximated more nearly to a semblance of the truth.' Cicero, op. cit., p. 383.

SELECT BIBLIOGRAPHY

A WORKS BY DAVID HUME

A Treatise of Human Nature (1739–40), edited by E. C. Mossner, Harmondsworth, 1969.

A Letter from a Gentleman to his friend in Edinburgh (1745), edited by E. C. Mossner and J. V. Price, Edinburgh, 1967.

Enquiries Concerning Human Understanding and Concerning the Principles of Morals (1777 edition), edited by L. A. Selby-Bigge, 3rd edition, revised by P. H. Nidditch, Oxford 1975.

Essays: Moral, Political and Literary (1777 edition), edited by E. F. Miller, Indianapolis, 1987.

The Natural History of Religion (1777 edition), edited by H. E. Root, Stanford, 1957.

B WORKS BY OTHER AUTHORS

Bayle, Pierre, *Historical and Critical Dictionary* (1697), selections translated by R. H. Popkin, Indianapolis, 1965.

Berkeley, George, *Principles of Human Knowledge, and Three Dialogues Between Hylas and Philonous*, edited by R. S. Woolhouse, London, 1988.

Cicero, Marcus Tullius, *De Natura Deorum*, translated by H. Rackham, London, 1933.

Clarke, Samuel, *A Demonstration of the Being and Attributes of God* (1705) and *A Discourse concerning the Unchangeable Obligations of Natural Religion* (1706), facsimile publication, Stuttgart-Bad Cannstatt, 1964.

Descartes, René, *The Philosophical Works of Descartes*, translated by E. S. Haldane and G. R. T. Ross, London, 1911.

Kemp Smith, Norman, *Hume's Dialogues Concerning Natural Religion*, edited with Introduction and Supplement, Edinburgh, 1947.

Labrousse, Elisabeth, *Bayle*, translated by D. Potts, Oxford, 1983.

Locke, John, *An Essay Concerning Human Understanding*, edited by P. H. Nidditch, Oxford, 1975.

Locke, John, *The Reasonableness of Christianity*, edited by G. W. Ewing, Chicago, 1965.

Malebranche, Nicolas, *The Search after Truth* (*De la recherche de la vérité*, 1674–5, 6th edition 1712), translated by T. M. Lennon and P. J. Olscamp, Columbus, 1980.

BIBLIOGRAPHY OF FURTHER READING

In addition to the edition of Hume's *Dialogues* by Kemp Smith, op. cit. above, the following editions each contain useful commentary by the editors:

Pike, Nelson, edited with commentary, Indianapolis, 1970.

Popkin, Richard, edited, together with *Of the Immortality of the Soul* and *Of Suicide*, Indianapolis, 1980.

Price, John V., edited, together with *The Natural History of Religion*, edited by A. W. Colver, Oxford 1976.

Gaskin, J. C. A., *Hume's Philosophy of Religion*, London, 1978. Deals with all Hume's writings on religion, from an analytic point of view.

Hall, R., *Fifty Years of Hume Scholarship: A Bibliographical Guide*, Edinburgh, 1978. Covers publications on Hume from 1925 to 1976. See entries in the index under 'Religion'.

Jeffner, A., *Butler and Hume on Religion*, Stockholm, 1966. A useful comparative analysis, with considerable historical material.

Jones, P., *Hume's Sentiments*, Edinburgh, 1982. An excellent, scholarly account of Hume's relations particularly to Cicero and French authors. Includes a fine chapter on scepticism in religion.

Mossner, E. C., *The Life of David Hume*, Oxford, 1970. The authoritative modern biography.

Popkin, R. H., *The History of Scepticism from Erasmus to Spinoza*, Berkeley, 1979. An indispensable scholarly study of the sceptical tradition, to which Hume belonged; essential for understanding religious scepticism and fideism.

Tweyman, S., *Scepticism and Belief in Hume's Dialogues Concerning Natural Religion*, Dordrecht, 1986. A detailed and interesting study making use of much recent research.